600 BC

The Departure of Lehi

A Landmark of Time

by Clay McConkie

CFI
Springville, Utah

BC 600

The Departure of Lehi

A Landmark of Time

ISBN 13: 978-1-55517-917-5

Published by CFI, an imprint of Cedar Fort, Inc., 2373 W. 700 S., Springville, UT, 84663
Distributed by Cedar Fort, Inc. www.cedarfort.com

Library of Congress Cataloging-in-Publication Data

McConkie, Clay.
600 B.C. : the departure of Lehi : a landmark of time and pivotal date in history / Clay McConkie.
p. cm.
ISBN 978-1-55517-917-5 (alk. paper)
1. Lehi (Book of Mormon figure) 2. Book of Mormon stories. 3. Book of Mormon--Geography. I. Title.

BX8627.4.L44M33 2007
289.3'22--dc22

2006039289

Cover design by Nicole Williams
Cover design © 2007 by Lyle Mortimer
Typeset by Kammi Rencher

Printed in the United States of America

10 9 8 7 6 5 4 3 2 1

Printed on acid-free paper

Table of Contents

PREFACE

600 b.c.

ON THE THIRD PAGE of the Book of Mormon, the second chapter and fourth verse, begins with a very simple sentence: "And it came to pass that he departed into the wilderness." The one speaking is Nephi, of course, and the person referred to is his father, the prophet Lehi.

At the bottom of the page is a footnote providing a date of departure, the exact time in history, according to Book of Mormon chronology, when Lehi left the city of Jerusalem and began an unusual journey. It is a very brief and unassuming date, but since the time it first appeared in print in 1830, the year of 600 BC has become a sign of recognition, not only heralding Lehi's departure, but more important, announcing the coming birth of Jesus Christ as well.

"And behold he cometh," the scripture says, "according to the words of the angel, in six hundred years from the time my father left Jerusalem."[1]

Many things were occurring in the Middle East and the Mediterranean areas during this period of time, and together these areas provide a historical backdrop to what was taking place when Lehi left the city. Being warned in a dream to flee for his life, he and his family packed their tents and provisions and departed into the desert, leaving forever their material wealth and the land of their inheritance. It was a historic occasion in the annals of the Book of Mormon, and yet one completely unnoticed by the surrounding nations.

But the event was significant, nevertheless, and all that was occurring shortly before and after the time of 600 BC forms an interesting and informative picture of that particular time period for eight specific areas of the world:

Judah	Media
Israel	Egypt
Assyria	Greece
Chaldea	Rome

Knowing what occurred elsewhere at the time that Lehi left Jerusalem puts the account in the Book of Mormon in a meaningful perspective. In the context of a Middle Eastern setting, as well as in places such as Egypt, Greece, and Rome, it is possible to view the early history of the Nephite record in a different way, one that brings together not only important events and circumstances but also an array of interesting personalities.

One of these figures was Zedekiah, the inexperienced 21-year-old king who was just beginning his reign in Jerusalem at the time of Lehi's departure. He was the final ruler in the kingdom of Judah and unfortunately the one who brought it to a close!

Chapter One

The Setting of 600 b.c.

Six hundred years before the birth of Christ, at a place near the city of Jerusalem, a man and his family began a historic journey. Logically it might have taken place at night when no one would see their departure, because this was not an ordinary occasion. The man was running for his life, trying to avoid those who earlier had threatened him and were now planning to kill him.

Like Jeremiah, Lehi was a prophet, and it was God who warned him in a vision to flee. It was necessary under the conditions to leave quickly and to take his family with him. So it was that, most likely under the cover of night, he left his homeland and the famous city of Jerusalem and silently departed into the wilderness.

Lehi's family at that time consisted of his wife and four sons, and the only things they took with them in their hurried flight were their tents and camels and a few possessions. They left their home and property behind, and in addition all of their gold and silver and precious things.

In the time of history it was in the commencement of the first year of the reign of Zedekiah, the last king to rule over the kingdom of Judah. The calendar date was 597 BC, but in the personal account kept by Lehi and his descendants, it was given as a different date, one which for centuries would be a landmark of time and a pivotal date in history.

It was in 600 BC, the family said, when they left the city and area of Jerusalem, six hundred years before the birth and advent of Jesus Christ. Often they used the date as a reference point in their writings.

"Yea, even six hundred years from the time that my father left Jerusalem," one of Lehi's sons wrote, "a prophet would the Lord God raise up among the Jews—even a Messiah, or, in other words, a Savior of the world."[2]

Certainly it was the date of 600 BC above all others in the history of Lehi that became a standard of measurement among those who came after him. It was this particular aspect of their heritage that helped set them apart as a unique civilization, though they were outcasts from Jerusalem and wanderers in a strange land.

And yet as far as history is concerned, it was in 597 BC, and not 600, that Lehi left the city. It was on the later date that the man known as Zedekiah acceded to the throne and became the king of Judah. Also in that year other important events were taking place, including an earlier invasion of the city of Jerusalem by the Chaldeans of Babylonia and the continuation of what eventually became known as the Babylonian Captivity or Exile.

Many centuries later a similar discrepancy of dates would arise in relation to the birth of Christ. Biblical scholars often affirm, for example, that Jesus was not born at the beginning of the first century AD, according to the present calendar, but instead several years earlier, anywhere from 1 BC to 8 BC. Since the more common estimate appears to be between the years 3 and 4, it is significant how this relates to the 600 BC date given by Lehi.

Just as Lehi's history places the accession of Zedekiah at 600 instead of 597, a discrepancy of three years, so also do modern biblical scholars set the birth of Christ at 3 or 4 BC, a difference in calendar date of approximately the same amount.

But whatever the correct answer to these situations might be, 600 BC still remains an important date in history. To the people who followed Lehi in the early sixth century, it was a time of genesis and hope, the beginning of a migration to a distant land of promise, as well as a profession of faith in the person known as Jesus Christ. Indeed it was this particular date that announced the exact time in the future when Jesus would be born at a place not far from Jerusalem.

Definitely the time of 600 BC is a historic landmark and pivotal point in time, not only for the departure of Lehi and his family but for many other significant events which were taking place. More important, it was a time when the hand of the Almighty manifested itself in an extraordinary way. It was one of those occasions when God chose to intervene at a certain time and place and significantly change the course of history. Yet in another sense, it was also a time of adventure and discovery, a time of resolution and dedication. And as the small group of pilgrims left their home near Jerusalem that day, most likely under cover of night and with a death threat hovering over their leader, it was a dramatic moment, heralding a new beginning for the family of Lehi and also a promise for the future in the coming birth of the Messiah!

Chapter Two

Departure into the Wilderness

When Lehi and his party left Jerusalem, they traveled toward the east to a place somewhere near the northern end of the Dead Sea, a distance of 20 to 30 miles. From there they turned south, paralleling the seacoast for another 50 miles, after which they traversed that part of the desert which was known as the Arabah. This was an inhospitable region of an additional 110 miles and has been referred to as a country so repelling that even people who lived nearby tried to avoid it.

The record of Lehi, being abridged and reported by his son Nephi, states that at this point they arrived at a mountainous area near the waters of the Red Sea. "And he came down by the borders near the shore of the Red Sea," Nephi writes, "and he traveled in the wilderness in the borders which are nearer the Red Sea. And he did travel in the wilderness with his family, which consisted of my mother, Sariah, and my elder brothers, who were Laman, Lemuel, and Sam."[3]

As to how long it took the group to get this far, the record does not say. However, the time spent in going from the end of the Arabah to a stopping place in a valley by a river of water, a distance estimated to be between 62 and 75 miles, was three days.

"And it came to pass that when he had traveled three days in the wilderness, he pitched his tent in a valley by the side of a river of water. And it came to pass that he built an altar of stones, and made an offering unto the Lord, and gave thanks unto the Lord our God."[4]

The total distance which Lehi traveled from Jerusalem, therefore, would appear to be about 250 miles. Corresponding travel time would then be eight or nine days, assuming a rate of speed by camels of approximately 28 to 30 miles a day.

Two hundred and fifty miles amounted to a considerable distance, especially in view of the fact that sometime after the party's arrival near the Red Sea, Nephi and his brothers returned to Jerusalem two different times. At the request of their father, they made the long journeys in order to obtain a record inscribed on brass plates and to bring back with them a man named Ishmael and his family. All together it amounted to at least 32 more days of traveling in the desert and the distance of a thousand miles.

In an initial reading of Lehi's record, as reported by his son, it is easy to get the idea that only three days of travel elapsed between Jerusalem and the Red Sea. "When he had traveled three days in the wilderness," he said, "he pitched his tent in a valley by the side of a river of water." And yet the actual distance involved rules out any such possibility. Since Lehi's group did not travel by foot but necessarily by way of camels, which was the conventional method of travel when tents and provisions were involved, a distance of 250 miles would normally require eight or nine days. This means that the three days of travel spoken of by Nephi refer only to the period of time after leaving the desert area known as the Arabah.

Caravan speeds in the desert at that time are said to have averaged from 28 to 30 miles a day with 40 being a maximum. Again this suggests the personal circumstances of Lehi as he traveled with his family in the wilderness.

From the valley by the river, which Lehi named the Valley of Lemuel, he and his family and the family of Ishmael eventually resumed their journey that took them down the entire length of the Arabian Peninsula. Most of this time they moved in a south-southeast direction and then turned toward the east, arriving at the shore of the Arabian Sea. Nephi's account at this point states that they had been traveling for eight years, and mentions no encounters they might have had with other people.

Once again a first reading of the record might give an inaccurate view of what actually took place. Lehi's party very likely did not always travel in privacy or anonymity, as might be supposed, nor did they go without any kind of itinerary, being led only by an instrument called the Liahona.

In actuality they probably followed a well-established route in the desert that had been used for centuries by merchants and traders, one which led to a specific destination where they could build a ship. At a final stopping place by the sea, there was not only access to necessary building materials but also possible assistance from experienced shipwrights who allegedly were in that area during this particular time period. It might be that Nephi obtained help from such people, in addition to information he received from the Lord.

Also as Lehi and his group moved down the Arabian Peninsula, they very possibly did not travel in obscurity but were often observed by other groups, including surrounding tribes through whose territory they were obliged to pass. It was not just a matter of going from place to place across hundreds of miles of wasteland, in other words, but at many stops along the way types of permission had to be obtained and the required payments given. Otherwise there would be a problem of personal safety and security, always a factor in desert travel.

The actual time that Lehi spent traveling between the Valley of Lemuel and the seacoast is also an important factor. It is obvious that eight years was an unusually long time for such a journey, one that a caravan traveling 30 miles a day could sometimes accomplish in three or four months. For whatever reasons, Lehi's group often stopped along the way, and evidently for long periods of time.

Certainly much happened on their trip that is not included in Nephi's record.

In retrospect, therefore, Lehi's flight into the wilderness proved to be an epic journey, and during the eight years that he and his party were in the desert, much was happening in the city of Jerusalem and the Kingdom of Judah, as well as in other places in the Middle East and the Mediterranean. Indeed it was a time of revolution and change, and also opportunity, in many different parts of the world. The sudden departure of a prophet from his homeland turned out to be an extremely significant occasion, from a religious viewpoint and a secular one as well, a pivotal time in history which brought into focus a veritable host of important people and events!

Chapter Three

Judah

Eleven years before Lehi left Jerusalem, a king of Judah named Josiah was slain in battle. This must have had a traumatic effect upon Lehi and his family because Josiah was one of the few Israelite rulers who reigned righteously.

At the time of his death, the king was in the area of Megiddo north of Jerusalem, trying to prevent Necho, the Egyptian pharaoh, from passing through his territory. Necho was on his way toward the north to help Assyria, which was at war with Chaldea and Media at the time, and although he warned Josiah not to interfere, it was to no avail and the king was killed.

Josiah had been Judah's ruler for thirty-one years and was an able administrator. His death in a seemingly unnecessary confrontation with Egypt was unfortunate, and people like Lehi, and also the prophet Jeremiah, were undoubtedly dismayed as some of Josiah's irresponsible sons began to emerge as successors to the throne.

The first of these was Jehoahaz, whom the people quickly anointed and crowned as king, although the hapless youth lasted only three months before Necho intervened and claimed the Kingdom of Judah as his own. The pharaoh replaced Jehoahaz with Eliakim, another son of Josiah, and changed his name to Jehoiakim. It was he who was the ruler in Judah for the next eleven years.

The accession of Jehoiakim to the throne provides an interesting backdrop for Lehi's later departure from Jerusalem. During the time that he was king, several events took place which undoubtedly affected the prophet and his family. The first of these was a sudden and heavy taxation forced upon the people.

As part of his administration, Necho of Egypt required a tribute of a hundred talents of silver and a talent of gold, which Jehoiakim secured by taxing the nobles who in turn got it from the commoners. It was a burdensome taxation, and the people suffered.

Prior to leaving Jerusalem, Lehi was apparently not living in the city itself but some distance outside the city walls. In any case he was still likely affected by Jehoiakim's taxation. The indications are that he was a wealthy man, possibly a merchant by trade, and had considerable influence in the community. His wealth consisted of "gold and silver and all manner of riches," including "precious things" that might have been brought in from distant places.

Lehi and his four sons, and also Sariah, were all witnesses to the dramatic events now taking place. Undoubtedly there were other children involved, although they are not mentioned by name, and as Jehoiakim began his rule as the new king of Judah in the closing years of the seventh century BC, Lehi's family might well have known that foreboding changes were occurring in their lives and that their future was uncertain.

This especially became evident in the year 605 BC when Egypt's authority over Judah was supplanted by that of people from Babylonia. The Chaldeans, led by a man named Nebuchadnezzar, defeated the forces of Assyria and Egypt in the Battle of Carchemish in the north, and like Necho a few years earlier, they now laid claim to the Kingdom of Judah.

The well-known event at Carchemish in 605 BC was noted specifically by the prophet Jeremiah: "The word of the Lord which came to Jeremiah the prophet against the Gentiles," he said, "against Egypt, against the army of Pharaoh-necho king of

Egypt, which was by the river Euphrates in Carchemish, which Nebuchadnezzar king of Babylon smote in the fourth year of Jehoiakim the son of Josiah king of Judah.

"Order ye the buckler and shield, and draw near to battle," the prophet continued. "Harness the horses and get up, ye horsemen, and stand forth with your helmets; furbish the spears, and put on the brigandines.

"Come up, ye horses; and rage, ye chariots; and let the mighty man come forth . . . For the Lord God of hosts hath a sacrifice in the north country by the river Euphrates."[5]

Unfortunately for the people of Judah and Jerusalem, having lost a favorite king in battle and then suffering conquests by the Egyptians and also the Chaldeans, the battle at Carchemish was a devastating occurrence. It was particularly discouraging when Nebuchadnezzar and his forces later entered Jerusalem and ransacked the precincts of the temple, taking sacred vessels for their own temple of Babylon in the land of Shinar.

"In the third year of the reign of Jehoiakim king of Judah came Nebuchadnezzar king of Babylon unto Jerusalem, and besieged it. And the Lord gave Jehoiakim king of Judah into his hand with part of the vessels of the house of God: which he carried into the land of Shinar to the house of his god; and he brought the vessels into the treasure house of his god."[6]

At this time Nebuchadnezzar was still a prince of Chaldea, the son of Nabopolassar the king. At some point following the Battle of Carchemish, however, he learned that his father had died, and when he came to Jerusalem, he was apparently on his way home for his coronation.

It was also while the Chaldeans were in the city that the first of three phases of the Babylonian Captivity took place. An undetermined number of people were taken captive, among whom were Daniel and his three friends spoken of in the Bible: Shadrach, Meshach, and Abednego. The unexpected removal of this first group of prisoners again must have prompted a premonition among many of the people and caused them to feel that future deportations might not be far away.

In the meantime, Jehoiakim continued as ruler of Judah, now a vassal of Chaldea instead of Egypt. No mention is made of any taxation or tribute, but the usual price of vassalage was undoubtedly present. Nebuchadnezzar expected Jehoiakim to perform according to all of his wishes, which at first the king consented to do, but youth and inexperience, in addition to a disreputable character, eventually proved to be to his disadvantage.

His disposition was not only to be unrighteous, as the Bible says, but also tended towards being capable of mischief and misconduct in his relationships with other people. From the beginning he seems to have been unsuited to be the king of Judah. Yet whatever his personality might have been, the young ruler after three years decided to rebel against Nebuchadnezzar, evidently thinking he could get assistance from Egypt. Then followed five years of harassment and invasion from a variety of nations abroad.

"And the Lord sent against him bands of the Chaldees, and bands of the Syrians, and bands of the Moabites, and bands of the children of Ammon, and sent them against Judah to destroy it, according to the word of the Lord."[7]

During these same years, the Lord sent messages to the people of Judah by way of prophets, including Jeremiah and others such as Lehi, who spoke out against the corruption of government and waywardness of the people. "And the Lord hath sent unto you all his servants the prophets," Jeremiah told them, "rising early and sending them; but ye have not hearkened, nor inclined your ear to hear."[8]

On one occasion, when Jeremiah was speaking to the people in the court of the temple, those present became angry and apprehended him. Whereas they had heretofore been patient and tolerant with his preaching, they now accused him openly of false accusations and threatened to kill him. The princes in the city, when they learned of the disturbance, also came to hear Jeremiah.

It was a tense situation in Jerusalem that day, "and all the people were gathered against Jeremiah in the house of the Lord . . . This man is worthy to die," the people shouted to the princes, "for he hath prophesied against this city, as ye have heard with your ears."[9]

But Jeremiah again stood before the congregation and condemned them for their ways and evil doings. Only if they repented of these things, he warned, would the Lord forego all that he had pronounced against them.

"As for me, behold, I am in your hand," he said. "Do with me as seemeth good and meet unto you. But know ye for certain, that if ye put me to death, ye shall surely bring innocent blood upon yourselves, and upon this city, and upon the inhabitants thereof: for of a truth the Lord hath sent me unto you to speak all these words in your ears."[10]

Then it was that the princes and most of the people spoke out in favor of Jeremiah. "This man is not worthy to die," they said, "for he hath spoken to us in the name of the Lord our God."[11]

Certainly it was an incident with which Lehi must have been familiar, and one also that fortunately turned out well for Jeremiah, something that would not always be true for him in the future. Nor was it so with another prophet named Urijah during this same time period.

Urijah prophesied in Judah and Jerusalem, saying basically the same things as Jeremiah. But in his regard, Jehoiakim, along with his nobles and princes, condemned Urijah to death. When Urijah heard of it, he was afraid, the scriptures say, and he fled into Egypt.

But Jehoiakim was angry and demanded his return. He ordered a man named Elnathan, the son of Achbor, to take certain men with him and go to Egypt and bring Urijah back. Then the king "slew him with the sword, and cast his dead body into the graves of the common people."[12]

Such was the case of one prophet but not of another, prompting the question of why there was a difference between someone like Urijah, as well as Lehi, and the prophet Jeremiah, Down through the difficult years while Jehoiakim was king, and even during the time of his successors, Jeremiah remarkably stayed alive while others were in danger.

Undoubtedly there were several reasons for the difference, but one had to do with a man named Ahikam, the son of Shaphan. At the time in the temple when most of the people, and surprisingly the princes also, decided in favor of Jeremiah's release, it was through the influence of Ahikam that it eventually took place. Again it was another instance where someone with recognition and authority came forward at the right moment, at a particular time and place, and provided needed assistance. Unfortunately, Urijah did not have this kind of support.

And as far as Lehi was concerned, the same also might be true. Over the years Jeremiah acquired the kind of connections which helped keep him free, those which socially and politically were to his advantage, but when Lehi appeared on the scene, he was not so fortunate and the people sought his life. It was at this time that the Lord himself intervened, however, and told the endangered prophet it was time for him to leave!

Chapter Four

Judah

Many things happened during the time of Jehoiakim, but it was sometime around the fourth year of his reign that two events took place which were particularly unusual. Possibly this was related to the fact that it was in the previous year that the young king had rebelled against Nebuchadnezzar.

One of these events concerned a group of people called the Rechabites who were descendants of Rechab. Jeremiah was instructed by the Lord to go to these people one day and invite them to the temple and give them wine to drink. It appeared to be an odd request, and no specific reason was given, but as things turned out, it proved to be an exercise in obedience.

As he had been commanded, the prophet placed pots full of wine before his guests and gave them cups from which to drink. But they quickly declined, saying that their father Jonadab, the son of Rechab, had earlier enjoined them to live an ascetic-type of life where they resided in tents rather than houses and abstained from certain kinds of food and drink, especially wine.

"Thus have we obeyed the voice of Jonadab, the son of Rechab our father," they told Jeremiah, "in all that he has charged us, to drink no wine all our days, we, our wives, our sons, nor our daughters; nor to build houses for us to dwell in; neither have we vineyard, nor field, nor seed: but we have dwelt in tents, and have obeyed, and done according to all that Jonadab our father commanded us."

But there had come a time, they said, when they moved from outlying places into the city. This occurred after they became afraid of the Chaldeans and Syrians who were threatening the lands of Judah with their invasions.

In consequence of these events, the Lord used the example of the Rechabites as a way of instructing the rebellious Israelites, comparing the obedience of one group with the disobedience of the other. He commended the first for performing the commandment of their father but severely condemned the second.

"Therefore thus saith the Lord God of hosts, the God of Israel," said Jeremiah: "Behold, I will bring upon Judah and upon all the inhabitants of Jerusalem all the evil I have pronounced against them; because I have spoken unto them, but they have not heard, and I have called unto them, but they have not answered."[13] It was not only a serious rebuke to the Israelites but a personal reprimand against the administration of Jehoiakim, against the misguided leader and his princes who were guiding the Kingdom of Judah toward destruction.

This also became increasingly evident in the unusual incident concerning the roll of a book, an event beginning in the fourth year of Jehoiakim and continuing into the fifth. Indeed, it is this detailed occurrence in the Bible which shows the eccentricity of the king and his unwillingness to accept any kind of divine instruction.

"Take thee a roll of a book," the Lord told Jeremiah, "and write therein all the words that I have spoken unto thee against Israel, and against Judah, and against all the nations, from the day I spake unto thee, from the days of Josiah, even unto this day."[14]

The prophet then instructed Baruch the scribe to do as the Lord commanded and record all of the revelations the prophet had received as he would dictate them. Undoubtedly this comprised a considerable amount of scripture. It is also interesting to note that Jeremiah stated at this time that he was being restricted, evidently being in some type of confinement which prevented him from going into the city.

"And Jeremiah commanded Baruch saying, I am shut up; I cannot go into the house of the Lord: therefore go thou, and read in the roll, which thou hast written from my mouth, the words of the Lord in the ears of the people in the Lords's house upon the fasting day: and also thou shalt read them in the ears of all Judah that come out of their cities."[15]

At this point, there commenced an unusual drama, all of which took place in the fifth year of the reign of Jehoiakim. A special fast was proclaimed at that time for all of the people in Jerusalem, as well as those who came from different cities throughout Judah. Within the walls of the temple, a meeting of the congregation was held, and in the place called the highest court, at the entry of the new gate, Baruch the scribe read to the people all the words of Jeremiah which had been recorded in the roll of the book.

One of those in the audience on that occasion was a man called Michaiah, and when he heard the book's contents, he immediately went to the residence of the king, to a certain chamber where the princes of the city were gathered. Three of these men were Elnathan the son of Achbor, and Delaiah and Gemariah. Michaiah then related to all of the princes what he had heard out of the book.

Elnathan had earlier acquired considerable notability in Jerusalem, for it was he who led a group of men to Egypt by Jehoiakim's command to bring back the prophet Urijah for execution. Apparently he was someone in a position of authority and leadership. But whatever his status might have been, Michaiah now related to him and the princes what he had heard in the temple.

Their reaction came quickly. Immediately they sent a man named Jehudi to Jeremiah's scribe and had him bring them the controversial book. "Sit down now," they told him, "and read it in our ears."[16]

The account in the Bible states that when the princes heard the prophecies of Jeremiah, they were fearful and decided among themselves that they should quickly tell the king. In the meantime they instructed Baruch to hide both himself and the prophet and let no one know of their whereabouts.

When Jehoiakim learned what had taken place, he ordered Jehudi to bring the roll and read it in front of him personally and before all of the princes. It was a critical time and an important moment of decision for the king. It was at this time that he definitely could have made a difference as to what would happen, not only to himself and to his people but to a kingdom as well. He had the opportunity, as would another king a short time ahead of him, to acknowledge the words of the Lord and prevent the approaching destruction of Judah.

Had he been old enough and wise enough like his father Josiah before him, he could have dramatically changed the course of history, but he was not that kind of person, and as a result things continued to go another way.

As Jehudi started reading from the roll of the book that day, he had not gone far before Jehoiakim suddenly took it from him and cut it with a knife "and cast it into the fire that was on the hearth, until all the roll was consumed." It was an abrupt occurrence and apparently had little effect on the princes in attendance, except Elnathan, Delaiah, and Gemariah, who earlier had encouraged the king not to abuse the roll. But the king ignored them and ordered that both Jeremiah and Baruch should be brought before him.[17]

The prophet was in hiding, however, and by commandment of the Lord composed another roll like the first, to which he added further prophecy. He then notified Jehoiakim that since he had chosen to burn the roll, neither he nor the city of Jerusalem would survive and all of the evil which had been pronounced against them would come to pass. It was a prediction that had been made many times before, but now with the destruction of a book of scripture, the prophecy was definitely sealed.

At this time Jeremiah also forecast the circumstances surrounding Jehoiakim's approaching death. Now he prophesied that his dead body would be "cast out in the day to the heat, and in the night to the frost."[18]

What happened next was inevitable although not entirely clear, either in the biblical text or in other information. Yet one thing was certain, and that was that Jehoiakim's tenure as king was coming to an end. His flagrant disregard for scripture and the dramatic way in which he burned the roll of the book soon brought things to a dramatic conclusion. There appeared to be a sense that something unusual was about to take place. Because of past events and circumstances, it could have been no other way, and when it finally did occur, a new era began in the affairs of the Kingdom of Judah and for the unfortunate inhabitants of Jerusalem!

CHAPTER FIVE

Judah

IN THE YEAR 597 BC, or in 600 according to the time reckoning of Lehi, Jehoiakim died after having ruled for eleven years. His administration had been a stormy one in which the government went from independence to Egyptian rule to Chaldean rule and finally to another attempt at independence with the hope of getting help from Egypt.

The Chaldeans from Babylonia were not about to relinquish hold upon their vassal state, however, and after several years of relative inactivity in the Judah area, Nebuchadnezzar and his armies again besieged the city of Jerusalem. Jehoiakim died, and his kingdom was temporarily given to his young son Jehoiachin.

One account has it that the Chaldeans killed the king and threw his body before the city walls without burial, seizing three thousand of the most important citizens and deporting them to Babylon. Yet other accounts, including those in the Bible as well as some given by modern historians, are more conservative in regard to the king's death and any prisoners that might have been taken.

The Bible itself refers to no captives at this time, and concerning Jehoiakim's death, the Book of 2 Kings says only that he "slept with his fathers." In 2 Chronicles the king reportedly was bound and prepared for deportation to Babylonia while sacred vessels were removed from the temple.

"Against him came up Nebuchadnezzar king of Babylon, and bound him in fetters, to carry him to Babylon. Nebuchadnezzar also carried of the vessels of the house of the Lord to Babylon, and put them in his temple."[19]

In addition there are the prophecies of Jeremiah, which mention Jehoiakim's corpse being cast out in the heat and frost and given the burial of an ass, along with other indications that the king was associated with one circumstance or another. Again it is a matter of speculation as to what actually happened, but whatever it was, it was undoubtedly a traumatic experience for him and the residents of Jerusalem, including Lehi and his family who as yet had not left the area.

Possibly the most important event on this particular occasion, aside from Jehoiakim's death, was the continuation of the Babylonian Captivity. With the end of one king's administration and the beginning of another, thousands were soon uprooted from their homes and removed to the place known as Babylon. Certainly it was a devastating time in the lives of people, and most of those who were taken captive probably knew they would never return.

When Nebuchadnezzar first entered Jerusalem following the battle of Carchemish, he had taken an undetermined number of prisoners, among whom were Daniel and his friends. At least some of the people deported at that time were a very select group, those "of the king's seed, and of the princes."

These were individuals like Daniel who were "well favored, and skilful in all wisdom, and cunning in knowledge, and understanding science, and such as had ability in them to stand in the king's palace, and whom they might teach the learning of the tongue of the Chaldeans."[20]

As Nebuchadnezzar came to Jerusalem the second time, however, he took another set of prisoners, possibly three thousand at the very beginning, but at least ten thousand, according to the

Bible, as he left the city, all of them part of the second phase of the Babylonian Captivity. Jehoiachin, the son of Jehoiakim, who had been king for only three months, submitted to the Chaldeans and was taken prisoner along with his immediate family and the chief rulers and officers of the kingdom. People in the military and those considered to be artisans and craftsmen were taken as well.

"And Jehoiachin the king of Judah went out to the king of Babylon, he, and his mother, and his servants, and his princes, and his officers: and the king of Babylon took him in the eighth year of his [Nebuchadnezzar's] reign. And he carried out thence all the treasures of the house of the Lord, and the treasures of the king's house, and cut in pieces all the vessels of gold which Solomon king of Israel had made in the temple of the Lord."

"And he carried away all Jerusalem, and all the princes, and all the mighty men of valor, even ten thousand captives, and all the craftsmen and smiths: none remained, save the poorest sort of the people of the land.

"And he carried away Jehoiachin to Babylon, and the king's mother, and the king's wives, and his officers, and the mighty of the land, those carried he into captivity from Jerusalem to Babylon. And all the men of might, even seven thousand, and craftsmen and smiths a thousand, all that were strong and apt for war, even them the king of Babylon brought captive to Babylon."[21]

In the place of Jehoiachin, the Chaldeans installed another son of Josiah as king. This was Mattaniah, whose name Nebuchadnezzar changed to Zedekiah. It was he who attempted to guide the affairs of Judah for the next eleven years, apparently with no intention of significantly deterring from the course of his predecessors. Even with the knowledge of what had happened to others, Zedekiah still continued in a reckless way.

In retrospect, and in regard to the last three kings, Jeremiah the prophet made fateful prophecies and predictions, referring first to Jehoahaz, also known as Shallum, the twenty-three-year old who succeeded his father Josiah. "For thus saith the Lord touching Shallum, the son of Josiah king of Judah," he said, "which reigned instead of Josiah his father, which went forth out of this place. He shall not return thither any more, but he shall die in the place whither they have led him captive and shall see this land no more."[22]

Next the prophet referred to Jehoiakim, mentioning that someday his dead body would "be buried with the burial of an ass, drawn and cast forth beyond the gates of Jerusalem."[23]

And finally he spoke of Coniah, or Jehoiachin, the ill-fated youth who ruled but briefly and was then carted off to Babylon. "As I live, saith the Lord," Jeremiah said, "though Coniah the son of Jehoiakim king of Judah were the signet upon my right hand, yet would I pluck thee thence;

"And I will give thee into the hand of them that seek thy life, and into the hand of them whose face thou fearest, even into the hand of Nebuchadnezzar king of Babylon, and into the hand of the Chaldeans. And I will cast thee out, and thy mother that bare thee, into another country, where ye were not born; and there shall ye die."[24]

Certainly it was a solemn indictment of the sons and grandson of Josiah, the king who earlier had ruled so well but whose posterity now was leading the Kingdom of Judah to destruction. Jehoiakim especially had been a disappointment, and his brother Zedekiah gave no indication that he would do any better. Indeed the final ruler of Judah would continue to make the same devastating mistakes his predecessors had made and eventually suffer a fate more tragic than them all!

Chapter Six

Judah

Nebuchadnezzar's deportation of ten thousand people in the time of Jehoiachin, and possibly three thousand earlier at the end of Jehoiakim's reign, produced radical changes in the capital city of Jerusalem and surrounding areas. These were not just political changes where one king replaced another, but social and economical changes as well. Most of those affected unfavorably appear to have been people in the upper classes, such as royalty, smiths, and craftsmen, along with "the mighty men of valor." "None remained," states the Bible, "save the poorest sort of the people of the land."[25]

The type of changes that occurred might well have been what one would expect in a situation where the social structure in a society was altered so quickly and drastically. Some of those who previously had been less prosperous and prominent now were able to obtain property which was left behind and consequently acquire new social status. This in turn had the potential of producing people who because of their new wealth and position became conceited and intolerant.

It is unlikely that Lehi obtained his wealth in such a way, yet one thing is evident, and that is that when the various deportations took place, he and undoubtedly others like him still remained in the Jerusalem area. There were certain people, in other words, besides those in the lower classes that were left behind, those who were able to escape the Babylonian juggernaut at least temporarily. Among these were Zedekiah, the heir apparent to the throne, and the ones who became his princes and officials.

In this latter group were the people who could have made a difference in preserving the Kingdom of Judah, important individuals who had the opportunity to exert a positive influence and provide the right kind of leadership. It was an opportune time for Zedekiah especially, had he been competent and willing to do what was necessary. One Israelite nation had already gone out of existence, yet there was still time for another to survive, and the responsibility for it happening rested heavily upon the king. Definitely it was a time of decision.

This was also the exact time when Lehi left Jerusalem. At some point during the first year of the reign of Zedekiah, being 600 BC by one calendar and 597 in another, the prophet and his family secretly left the city and began a long journey to a promised land, one that would involve several years of travel in the wilderness and finally a voyage across the ocean. Behind him he left his home and occupation and his accumulated wealth. It was a lot for any man to give up. But in a way that was terribly significant, Lehi also left a city, the unfortunate capital of Judah, which was condemned and scheduled for destruction unless something miraculous took place in the near future that would prevent it.

When Nebuchadnezzar came to Jerusalem and established Zedekiah as the new ruler, he took an oath of him and made a covenant that things would take place according to a Chaldean plan. Unquestionably there was to be complete obedience from the new king, which entailed allegiance to the Babylonians only and no correspondence with other nations, particularly nearby Egypt. If Zedekiah had done this one thing, accepting a plan that the prophet Jeremiah approved of and endorsed, Judah possibly would have continued as a nation under the auspices of another system of government, such as that of Persia, and had a much different future.

But from the beginning Zedekiah was indecisive, being strongly influenced by his princes and advisers, and even though he periodically consulted with Jeremiah, in the end it became increasingly evident that like his immediate predecessors, he was incompetent and incapable of being king. His various sons, if they ever had any hopes of succeeding him, would tragically be disappointed. As it turned out, only one of them was destined to escape the disaster that lay ahead.

A primary figure during this period of time was undoubtedly Jeremiah the prophet. As one who was sympathetic to the pro-Babylonian party in Jerusalem, as opposed to those who were pro-Egyptian, he consistently advocated submission to the forces of Nebuchadnezzar. Even though it meant a loss of political independence, there was no other way under the circumstances to escape conquest and annihilation. Time after time the prophet emphasized this, and on occasion Zedekiah seemed to listen, but unfortunately he was too much under the control of those who surrounded him. Before Lehi left Jerusalem, an event which was now imminent or had already taken place, he among others must have sensed that the voice of a prophet, even that of Jeremiah, was not apt to be taken seriously by those who were in the government.

In the meantime, important events were occurring in the Middle East. Approximately four years after Lehi's departure, the pharaoh Necho of Egypt died, and his son Psamtik II took his place, a situation causing an immediate effect on Judah and surrounding nations. Reportedly, a summit meeting, as it might be called, was held in Jerusalem in which ambassadors from Ammon, Moab, Edom, Tyre, and Sidon were in attendance. The purpose of the meeting was to discuss the implications of what had happened in Egypt and how it affected Judah and its neighbors. Undoubtedly the chief concern was how to proceed in regard to the king of Babylon.[26]

The new Egyptian pharaoh was noted for his military prowess, and as an ally to a coalition of forces he would be an invaluable benefit. Consequently, one topic of the summit very likely was related to rebellion and insurrection, it being an important option.

It was during this same time period that the prophet Jeremiah sent letters to the kings who were represented at the summit. Indeed he sent messages to Ammon, Moab, and Edom in the south and east and to Tyre and Sidon on the Mediterranean coast. In all of these messages he quoted the Lord as saying that Nebuchadnezzar was acceptable in his eyes and indeed was his "servant." "And now I have given all of these lands into the hand of Nebuchadnezzar king of Babylon, my servant," the Lord said, "and the beasts of the field have I given him also to serve him."[27]

The ones who resisted this unusual injunction and would not comply were to face punishment by the sword, as well as by famine and pestilence. Such a sentence would continue until the countries involved were consumed. "But the nations that bring their neck under the yoke of the king of Babylon, and serve him," the Lord promised, "those will I let remain still in their own land."[28]

In addition to the letters, Jeremiah also spoke to Zedekiah personally, saying "Bring your necks under the yoke of the king of Babylon, and serve him and his people, and live. Why will ye die, thou and thy people, by the sword, by the famine, and by the pestilence, as the Lord hath spoken against the nation that will not serve the king of Babylon?"[29]

On this same occasion, as a prelude to the approaching devastation, the prophet referred to certain articles in the temple that had not been taken during the last invasion. These were the pillars, bases, and residue of vessels that still remained, along with the so-called sea, a large vat or basin that had once rested on the backs of twelve bronze oxen.

The sacred vessels, Jeremiah said, in both the temple and the palace of the king, would all be confiscated by invading armies. As for the sea, bases, and pillars, they were eventually broken in pieces and the metal transported to Babylon.

All of these events occurred in the vicinity of 593 BC, the fourth and fifth years of the reign of Zedekiah. Moreover, it was at this same time that the king made an important trip to the Chaldean capital to see Nebuchadnezzar. It is not stated what his purpose was, but supposedly it was to pay the periodic tribute and declare continuing allegiance to the Babylonian king. He was accompanied on the trip by a man named Seraiah, whom the Bible characterizes as a "quiet prince."

Before Seraiah left, Jeremiah conferred with him and gave him certain instructions. The prophet had written earlier a lengthy commentary on what would eventually happen to Nebuchadnezzar and the Babylonians, one that did not necessarily advocate support for the Babylonian king at this time but stated in detail how one day in the future his government would come to an end. He commanded Seraiah to take the commentary with him and upon arriving in Babylon read it aloud. The Bible does not say to whom, but in part at least it was likely meant for those in captivity who would welcome any news that someday their captors would be defeated.

Jeremiah then instructed Seraiah to bind a stone to the commentary and eventually cast it into the Euphrates River. "And thou shalt say," he told him, speaking for the Lord, "thus shall Babylon sink, and shall not rise from the evil that I will bring upon her."[30]

It is significant that Zedekiah and Seraiah traveled to Babylon at this particular time, so soon after the summit meeting of ambassadors in Jerusalem. The implication is strong that the king was moving increasingly toward the idea of rebellion, and the visit to Nebuchadnezzar was likely not one of true allegiance but only a pretense. In any case, the situation in Judah was becoming more uncertain and dangerous. Definitely it was an important time of decision for Zedekiah, because any move he now made in the wrong direction would not just endanger the Kingdom of Judah but potentially bring about its entire destruction!

Chapter Seven

Judah

During the time of the Jerusalem summit, either shortly before or after, Jeremiah wrote a letter to the people in Babylon who had been taken captive, telling them to be patient where they were and encouraging them to lead normal lives. Despite what others said, he told them, including statements from false prophets and diviners, their future release would not be for another seventy years.

"Build ye houses and dwell in them," he counseled, speaking for the Lord, "and plant gardens, and eat the fruit of them. Take ye wives, and beget sons and daughters; and take wives for your sons, and give your daughters to husbands, that they may bear sons and daughters, that ye may be increased there, and not diminished. And seek the peace of the city whither I have caused you to be carried away captives, and pray unto the Lord for it; for in the peace thereof shall ye have peace."[31]

But information was definitely given that their captivity would continue. "For thus saith the Lord," Jeremiah said, "that after seventy years be accomplished at Babylon I will visit you and perform my good word toward you, in causing you to return to this place."[32]

The problem was that unauthorized people, both in Jerusalem and Babylon, were speaking as though they had been called as prophets. One of these was a man named Hananiah who talked with Jeremiah in the temple one day in the presence of priests and some of the people who had gathered there.

According to Hananiah, the Babylonian Captivity was only temporary and would end within two years. At that time Jehoiachin and his people would return, he said, bringing with them all of the temple vessels that had been seized by Nebuchadnezzar. It was an optimistic prophecy and prediction, one that people liked to hear, but even though many believed that Jehoiachin was still the legitimate king and hoped he would return, it was the words of Jeremiah that ultimately prevailed.

The prophet censured Hananiah for acting without authority and causing people to trust in a lie. He prophesied that as a result of what he had done, he would be punished and cast "from off the face of the earth." "This year thou shalt die," Jeremiah told him, "because thou hast taught rebellion against the Lord."[33] And as predicted, it was during the same year, as recorded in the Bible, that Hananiah died.

There were others besides Hananiah who made similar predictions and prophecies. Three of these were Ahab, Zedekiah, and Shemaiah, all captives in Babylon. All were censured by Jeremiah and given dire predictions, but the latter especially was criticized because he had sent damaging letters to the priests and people in Jerusalem, engaging in further rebellion against the Lord.

The time which elapsed during the next two years was crucial as people waited to see if Hananiah's prophecy would come true. And when it never materialized, a new feeling and atmosphere pervaded the capital city. It was apparently soon after this that Zedekiah finally made his decision to solicit help from the Egyptians and rebel against Nebuchadnezzar. About the same time, the pharaoh Psamtik II died, and the one known in the Bible as Hophra replaced him.

Whatever it was that caused Zedekiah to rebel, it is evident that he had obtained some kind of understanding and alliance with Egypt and was depending on the pharaoh for help. There is no indication that any of the other summit nations joined him, although people falling away to the Chaldeans resorted to some of these places for refuge, and consequently as things turned out, the Israelite king ended up on his own. It was an unfortunate situation for him, and in the ninth year of his reign, Nebuchadnezzar again invaded the Kingdom of Judah.

In the conflict that followed, the cities throughout Judah fell one by one until only Jerusalem along with Lachish and Azekah remained. It appeared that there would be a total conquest this time, and it prompted Zedekiah to send two messengers to the prophet Jeremiah asking for help. These men were Pashur and Zephaniah, a priest.

"Enquire, I pray thee, of the Lord for us," they said, speaking for the king, "for Nebuchadnezzar king of Babylon maketh war against us; if so be that the Lord will deal with us according to all his wondrous works, that he may go up from us."[34]

Despite all of the warning and advice given by Jeremiah in the past, Zedekiah still continued to ask the Lord for help, but the prophet again made it clear what the Lord's position was and what the prospects were for the future.

"Behold, I will turn back the weapons of war that are in your hands," the Lord said, "wherewith ye fight against the king of Babylon, and against the Chaldeans, which besiege you without the walls, and I will assemble them into the midst of this city. And I myself will fight against you with an outstretched hand and with a strong arm, even in anger, and in fury, and in great wrath. And I will smite the inhabitants of this city, both man and beast: they shall die of a great pestilence."[35]

The Lord then described how he would deliver the king and his servants, and the surviving population, into the hands of the king of Babylon, where there would be no pity or mercy. This time there would be a complete destruction of the nation. And yet there were still two options, as there had always been. "I set before you the way of life," the Lord stated, "and the way of death."

"He that abideth in this city shall die by the sword, and by the famine, and by the pestilence: but he that goeth out, and falleth to the Chaldeans that besiege you, he shall live, and his life shall be unto him for a prey. For I have set my face against this city for evil, and not for good, saith the Lord: it shall be given into the hand of the king of Babylon, and he shall burn it with fire."[36]

Certainly this had been Jeremiah's counsel from the beginning: Fall away to the Chaldeans, he said, and be saved. And undoubtedly there were those who did this in order to avoid the disaster which lay ahead. But it was not necessarily a popular thing to do, nor was it always possible since those in authority were observing carefully who was leaving and entering the city.

On another occasion during the Chaldean siege, Zedekiah once more sent messengers to Jeremiah, this time a man named Jehucal and again Zephaniah the priest. It was during a crucial and significant stage of the war in which the Chaldeans withdrew temporarily as Pharaoh's army finally arrived from Egypt, supposedly to encounter Nebuchadnezzar. It is also here in the biblical account where it states that Jeremiah, at least during this particular time period, had not yet been put in prison.

"Pray now unto the Lord our God for us," the messengers said to the prophet, again speaking in behalf of the king. It was at least the second time that such a request had been made to the Lord, and the answer was still the same. Moreover, Jeremiah specifically made it known what the result of Egypt's recent appearance would be.[37]

"Thus shall ye say to the king of Judah, that sent you unto me to enquire of me," the prophet said. "Behold, Pharaoh's army, which is come forth to help you, shall return to Egypt into their own land. And the Chaldeans shall come again and fight against this city, and take it, and burn it with fire.

"Thus saith the Lord; Deceive not yourselves, saying, The

Chaldeans shall surely depart from us: for they shall not depart. For though ye had smitten the whole army of the Chaldeans that fight against you, and there remained but wounded men among them, yet should they rise up every man in his tent and burn this city with fire."[38]

It was an ominous forecast, and not an easy one for Zedekiah to hear, and yet it should not have been too much of a surprise for the beleaguered king, since he had been warned of it so many times before. But now that the final days of the kingdom were drawing closer, he must have had more than just a premonition of what was about to happen.

It was also on this occasion, for the purpose of separating himself "in the midst of the people," that Jeremiah attempted to leave the city. His intention was to travel north into the land of Benjamin, his home area, but at the gate of exit he was arrested by the captain in charge and accused of falling away to the Chaldeans. The prophet denied it but nevertheless was taken to the king's princes who "smote him and put him in prison." In the house of a man called Jonathan the scribe, where a type of dungeon with cells had been constructed, they confined Jeremiah for many days.

Sometime after Lehi had left Jerusalem, at a time when his sons returned briefly to the city, Nephi made a statement that Jeremiah had been cast into prison.[39] This must have happened before the rebellion of Zedekiah and the invasion of Judah, although it is not mentioned in the Bible. Earlier Jeremiah had been placed in the stocks for a day, and it is possible that on another occasion he could have also been imprisoned for a brief time. But the more lengthy imprisonment which now took place was to last indefinitely until Jerusalem finally fell to the invaders.

Zedekiah eventually sent for Jeremiah and had him brought to the king's palace. In secret he asked the prophet if there was "any word from the Lord." And again Jeremiah said there was, which was that the king would definitely "be delivered into the hand of the king of Babylon." He also inquired why he had been imprisoned unjustly and asked where the false prophets were who had said Judah would not be invaded. Then he solicited the king that he not be sent back to the dungeon, for he feared he would die there.[40]

Zedekiah consequently placed Jeremiah in the court of the prison, located at a place inside the palace, and ordered that the prophet be given daily "a piece of bread out of the bakers street, until all the bread in the city were spent." Indeed such a declaration at this time, in this particular part of the siege, suggested strongly that the fall of the city was not too far distant.[41]

Jeremiah's new location, however, was only temporary. After a brief time, certain of the princes went to the king and reminded him how the prophet had continually encouraged people to fall away to the Chaldeans, thus interfering with the efforts of the military and inciting uncertainty and discontent among the people. They brashly insisted that Jeremiah be put to death, and in response the insecure and vacillating Zedekiah said, "Behold, he is in your hand: for the king is not he that can do any thing against you."[42]

The Bible is very brief sometimes in describing certain situations and circumstances, but it is revealing to see how Zedekiah acted this time, going from one stance and viewpoint to another so quickly. Obviously the princes might have revolted and taken over the government, had he not acted as he did, but whatever the conditions, the king impulsively made another decision, one among many that was gradually leading him and the others to a point of annihilation.

The princes, however, wasted little time in dealing with Jeremiah. They transported him to another area in the court of the prison, to a dungeon called the dungeon of Malchiah, and there let him down with cords where the prophet sank into the mire. He remained in that condition for an undetermined length of time before a man named Ebedmelech came to his rescue.

As one of the eunuchs in the king's palace, Ebedmelech must have been someone with considerable authority, or at least one who was willing to take action that would free Jeremiah, despite the threat it would undoubtedly incur from the princes. He left the palace and went to the gate of Benjamin, the place of exit where earlier the prophet had been arrested. He knew the king was sitting there, and he implored him strongly on behalf of Jeremiah.

"My Lord the king," he said, "these men have done evil in all that they have done to Jeremiah the prophet, whom they have cast into the dungeon; and he is like to die for hunger in the place where he is: for there is no more bread in the city."[43]

Not surprisingly, Zedekiah again was easy to entreat, and just as readily as he had given in to the princes, he now acquiesced to Ebedmelech, telling him to take thirty men and go to the dungeon and release Jeremiah. The drama that took place at this time, although very briefly described in the Bible, is one of the most dramatic incidents in Israelite history. Certainly it was a tribute to the man who risked his life to befriend a prophet, at the same time showing allegiance to God as well.

When Ebedmelech and the thirty men went to the dungeon that day, they fashioned cords out of "old cast clouts and old rotten rags" and dropped them down to Jeremiah in the mire. "Put now these old cast clouts and rotten rags under thine armholes under the cords," they said. Then they drew up the prophet and again took him back to the court of the prison.[44]

It was sometime later that the Lord would speak to Jeremiah saying, "Go and speak to Ebedmelech the Ethiopian, saying, Thus saith the Lord of Hosts, the God of Israel: Behold, I will bring my words upon this city for evil, and not for good, and they shall be accomplished in that day before thee. But I will deliver thee in that day, saith the Lord: and thou shalt not be given into the hand of the men of whom thou art afraid.

"For I will surely deliver thee," he told him, "and thou shalt not fall by the sword, but thy life shall be for a prey unto thee: because thou hast put thy trust in me, saith the Lord."[45]

Following his release from the dungeon, Jeremiah had again been taken to the court of the prison. Once more the king sent for him, this time meeting him in the temple in the place referred to as the third entry. "I will ask thee a thing," Zedekiah said, wanting to know if the Lord had revealed anything new. "Hide nothing from me."[46]

Jeremiah knew what Zedekiah's responses had been in the past and how reluctant he had been to take advice. He also remembered how the princes had threatened the prophet personally and persuaded the king to cast him into the dungeon.

"As the Lord liveth," Zedekiah told him, "I will not put thee to death, neither will I give thee into the hand of these men that seek thy life."[47]

Jeremiah then spoke as he had done several times before, saying that all Zedekiah needed to do was to "go forth unto the king of Babylon's princes" and he would be saved, he and all who were in the city of Jerusalem. Otherwise the city would be destroyed and everything in it burned with fire.[48]

But Zedekiah again was fearful. "I am afraid of the Jews that are fallen to the Chaldeans," he said, "lest they deliver me into their hand, and they mock me." He then cautioned the prophet, telling him to say nothing to the princes concerning his visit, unless they had questions, and then to say only that he had asked not to be sent back to the prison in the house of Jonathan the scribe, lest he die there.[49]

Surely these were fateful words of a confused and bewildered king who a short time later in the eleventh year of his reign finally saw the city of Jerusalem broken up. In the fourth month and the ninth day of that year, the Chaldean armies finally breached the walls of the city. According to the Bible, the six main officers of the king of Babylon proudly entered the city and sat in the middle gate, along with the residue of the princes. Jerusalem had been under siege for eighteen months, its eventual demise being inevitable, and now as the invading forces made their triumphant entry, the Kingdom of Judah virtually came to an end. The unfortunate Zedekiah had failed to listen to Jeremiah and the prophets one last time, and with the mighty men of war who chose to follow him, the king fled from the city by night and headed toward the plains of Jericho!

Chapter Eight

Judah

It was on the ninth day of the fourth month during the eleventh year of Zedekiah's reign that Jerusalem and the Kingdom of Judah succumbed to the invading armies of Nebuchadnezzar. The fateful year was 586 BC, and as predicted by the Lord and his prophet, the enemy showed no pity or mercy. In his flight to Jericho east of the city, Zedekiah was soon overtaken by the Chaldeans, and his soldiers were scattered from him.

The custom of the Chaldean king was not always to be personally involved when besieging and entering a city. Often he would stay at Riblah which was north of Jerusalem and there regulate the affairs of his armies. At the time that Jerusalem was conquered, therefore, Nebuchadnezzar was at his northern base and stronghold when Zedekiah, along with his family and princes, was brought before him.

The account of Zedekiah's encounter with Nebuchadnezzar, as recorded in the Bible, is brief, saying only that the Chaldean king passed judgment on him and then slew all of his sons before him, as well as his princes and nobles. He then put out the king's eyes "and bound him with chains, to carry him to Babylon."[50]

Such was the fate of Zedekiah, the last of twenty kings who ruled the Kingdom of Judah and who now was carried to the place in Babylonia where he would spend the rest of his life in prison. Behind he left a city that was defeated and broken and in the hands of the enemy, and within one month after Jerusalem fell, Nebuchadnezzar turned the control of his army over to a man named Nebuzaradan, a captain of the guard.

Meanwhile in Babylon, near the River Cheber where some of the Israelite captives were living, the prophet Ezekiel had nothing but unkind words for Zedekiah, reprimanding him for his conduct in breaking the oath and covenant he had made with Nebuchadnezzar. "He rebelled against him," he said, "in sending his ambassadors into Egypt, that they might give him horses and much people."

"As I live, saith the Lord God, surely in the place where the king dwelleth that made him king, whose oath he despised, and whose covenant he brake, even with him in the midst of Babylon he shall die. Neither shall Pharaoh with his mighty army and great company make for him in the war, by casting up mounts, and building forts, to cut off many persons.

"Seeing he despised the oath by breaking the covenant, when lo, he had given his hand, and hath done all these things, he shall not escape. Therefore thus saith the Lord God; As I live, surely mine oath that he hath despised, and my covenant that he hath broken, even it will I recompense upon his own head."[51]

In Jerusalem, therefore, in the wake of all that had happened, the new commander of the Chaldean army quickly and methodically burned the temple of Solomon, which had stood for more than four hundred years, followed by Zedekiah's palace and the royal residences of the princes and nobles. "Every great man's house burnt he with fire."[52] Eventually all of the houses in the great city of Jerusalem were destroyed in the holocaust. And finally Nebuzaradan gave the order for the city walls to be torn down.

It was also during this time that certain people were taken captive and assembled in the city. These included Seraiah and Zephaniah, who were the two chief priests, three keepers of the door, an officer or eunuch that had been over the men of war, several people in the personal service of the king, the principal scribe, "and threescore men of the people of the land, that were found in the city." All of these Nebuzaradan took to Nebuchadnezzar in Riblah where the Chaldean king executed them.[53]

"Now the rest of the people that were left in the city, and the fugitives that fell away to the king of Babylon, with the remnant of the multitude, did Nebuzaradan the captain of the guard carry away. But the captain of the guard left of the poor of the land to be vinedressers and husbandmen."[54]

Prior to the burning of the temple, the Chaldeans plundered its interior and removed everything of value. They took the two giant pillars of brass or bronze that stood in the porch at the temple's entrance and broke them in pieces, preparing the metal for shipment to Babylon. Also the huge vat or basin known as the "molten sea," which once rested on the backs of twelve brazen oxen, was dismantled and taken.

"The caldrons also," states the Bible, "and the shovels, and the snuffers, and the bowls, and the spoons, and all the vessels of brass wherewith they ministered, took they away. And the basons, and the firepans, and the bowls, and the caldrons, and the candlesticks, and the spoons, and the cups; that which was of gold in gold and that which was of silver in silver, took the captain of the guard away."[55]

Certainly this was a sacrilege and catastrophe for the conquered people of Judah. The city of Jerusalem, the place where God's name once was, lay in smoldering ruins. Now the people had no king or temple or nation. The house of Israel, having been partially removed more than a century before, was now completely dismembered and the members of a once proud body scattered to many different parts of the world.

There was one bright spot, however, in the middle of all the chaos and confusion. The prophet Jeremiah, who had been in the court of the prison for an undetermined length of time, was finally released and given his freedom. It is uncertain what the exact circumstances were, but the Chaldeans eventually rejected the idea of any kind of penalty or imprisonment and told the prophet he could go wherever it was good or convenient for him to go.

One of the biblical accounts states that Nebuzaradan sent certain of the princes to the court of the prison where they released Jeremiah and after a time committed him to the care of a man named Gedaliah.[56] Earlier Nebuchadnezzar had given permission to free the prophet, yet the alleged action of the princes is in apparent contradiction of another account in the Bible which says that the he was actually out of prison at the time of his release and on his way to Babylon as a captive.

In the second account, it was Nebuzaradan himself who released Jeremiah after receiving permission from Nebuchadnezzar. "Take him and look well to him, and do him no harm," the Chaldean king said, "and do unto him even as he shall say unto thee." It was then that the captain of the guard went to the nearby city of Ramah, a place where captives were temporarily assembled before being transported to Babylon.[57]

Jeremiah was in chains there, and Nebuzaradan ordered that he be released. "The Lord thy God hath pronounced this evil upon this place," he told the prophet. "Now the Lord hath brought it, and done according as he hath said; because ye have sinned against the Lord, and have not obeyed his voice, therefore this thing is come upon you."

Then followed the words of the conqueror, again including some of the most impressive statements ever recorded in the Bible as Nebuzaradan removed Jeremiah's chains and set him free. "And now, behold, I loose thee this day from the chains which were upon thine head," he said. "If it seem good unto thee to come with me into Babylon, come; and I will look well unto thee: but if it seem ill unto thee to come with me into Babylon, forbear: behold, all the land is before thee: whither it seemeth good and convenient for thee to go, thither go."

Finally he instructed the prophet to go to Gedaliah who had been made governor over the cities of Judah. "Or go wheresoever it seemeth convenient unto thee to go," he said once again.[58] Then Nebuzaradan gave him some food and a reward and released him.

In the meantime, somewhere in the distance at a place located on the American continent, and at a time not too long after the destruction of Jerusalem, the prophet Lehi in speaking to members of his family gave them the inevitable news. "For behold, said he, I have seen a vision, in which I know that Jerusalem is destroyed; and had we remained in Jerusalem we should also have perished."[59] Surely it was a tragic epitaph to all that had happened, and with the unfortunate destruction of Judah's capital city, and an even more tragic end to a kingdom, a long and historic era came to a close!

Chapter Nine

Israel

More than a hundred years before Jerusalem fell, another Israelite kingdom had been conquered and its capital devastated. In the year 721 BC, the armies of the Assyrian Empire led by Sargon II defeated and occupied the city of Samaria, the beleaguered capital of the Kingdom of Israel. Prior to that time, during the days of Saul, David, and Solomon, the combined Israelites had been a single independent nation before dividing into the two separate kingdoms of Israel and Judah.

Being the first kingdom to be conquered, many of the inhabitants of the Kingdom of Israel were deported to Assyria and adjoining areas. Vast deportations had occurred earlier in about 733 BC, when captives were taken from northern Palestine and Transjordan, and then in the year 721, or soon thereafter, thousands more were evacuated from the central part of Palestine. It was a discouraging time for the Israelite people, who long had prized their independence.

The policy of the Assyrian Empire at this time was to deport only about one-half of a conquered population, and sometimes less, bringing in foreign colonists to take their place. Those taken captive, which included members of the military and people in the upper classes, along with some who were in skilled occupations, were taken to cities such as Haran, Guzana, Halah, and Ninevah in present-day Syria and Iraq, as well as places further east in Media, now known as Iran. Here they remained for more than a hundred years until the end of the seventh century BC when the empire of Assyria collapsed and the political situation in the Middle East suddenly began to change. Certainly it is significant that sometime during this general time period, at least part of those taken captive from the Kingdom of Israel left their places of captivity for whatever reason and migrated into what has been referred to in scripture as the "land of the north" or the "north countries."

In a time of history when Assyria had passed through the most successful days of its empire (744–627 BC), extending through the successive reigns of Tiglath-Pileser, Shalmaneser, Sargon, Sennacherib, Esarhaddon, and Ashurbanipal, it now faced annihilation. In 614 BC the key city of Ashur fell to foreign invaders, and finally in the year 612, the capital city of Nineveh was besieged and destroyed. Again it was apparently sometime during this period of time, when the golden age of Assyrian kings had passed and weaker rulers took their place, that an undetermined number of Israelite captives left the confines of Assyria and began a long journey to the north.

Their objective was to leave their present location and travel to an entirely different area where they could be isolated from other people. They were dissatisfied with how they had lived in the past, not having kept certain religious rules and commandments, and their intent now was to enter a new kind of life and future. Indeed it appeared that this specific group of people was being prepared by God himself for an unusual destiny, one that would ultimately take them to a very unexpected place within the confines of the earth.

The only documentation which refers to this event is the noncanonical scripture known as the Apocrypha, where, in the Book of Second Esdras, it describes how the ten tribes of Israel were captured by the Assyrians and taken into captivity. It was there that some of them eventually made their decision to leave.

"But they formed this plan for themselves," the record says, "that they would leave the multitude of the nations and go to a more distant region where mankind had never lived, that there at least they might keep their statutes which they had not kept in their own land."

At that point in history, according to the apocryphal account, it was the Most High who supported the migration and was guiding the people. He it was who took them to a prescribed location where some divine purpose could be accomplished. Other than just going to a new locality, there was also the idea that a more religious reason or motive was involved.

"And they went in by the narrow passages of the Euphrates River," the record continues. "For at that time the Most High performed signs for them and stopped the channels of the river until they had passed over." Then the scripture gives a brief and scanty report of where they were going. "Through that region there was a long way to go, a journey of a year and a half; and that country is called Arzareth."[60]

The meaning of the word Arzareth in Hebrew is "another land," not much of a clue as to location, but reference to eighteen months of travel would suggest a penetration of territory as far north as Scandinavia or northern Asia. And whatever the type of geography might have been, there is definitely an implication that much more than just ordinary circumstances was involved. Given the information supplied by the Apocrypha, as well as that which was acquired at a later time, the idea is that something of unusual significance was taking place.

In approximately 600 BC, in fact, soon after the destruction of Nineveh and about the same time that the prophet Lehi and his party left Jerusalem, something of monumental importance allegedly occurred in the northern part of the globe. At a latitude well beyond familiar places in the Middle East and Mesopotamia, a drama very briefly alluded to in scripture but at the same time fraught with unusual implications was being played out in a northern clime that was unmapped and unexplored. In a distant place where rock and ice often mark the landscape, a group of people emanating from the former Kingdom of Israel and the ten tribes finally arrived at a certain destination in "the north countries" and then quietly and unobserved by other people mysteriously disappeared!

Chapter Ten

Israel

What actually happened to the migrating tribes after they had traveled through Arzareth is unknown. Their sudden disappearance definitely remains a mystery. An actual disappearance, however, is still open to question since it is believed by some that the tribes upon arriving at their destination in the north eventually dispersed and intermingled with other people. Over a long period of time, in other words, they were disseminated and incorporated with surrounding nations.

The majority of public opinion among those familiar with the ten tribes very likely would share this point of view. One poll, to cite an example, showed that out of more than 200 people who responded to a survey, fifty-three percent said that the tribes were currently dispersed among the different countries. Twenty-nine percent thought they were in a condition similar to the City of Enoch and had been taken to some other planet or sphere, while eleven percent favored a north pole theory in which people were hidden somewhere in arctic or polar regions. Four percent believed they were in a hollow earth situation, and two percent had theories of their own.[61]

But wherever the ten tribes are at present, meaning their descendants and posterity, their actual condition or whereabouts will probably never be known until there is some kind of new information or divine revelation. Since it is alleged that the people involved were guided by God from the beginning, only He can say for certain what it was that actually happened to them. In the meantime there will always be a question, along with the inevitable plethora of theory and speculation.

And yet history itself can maybe provide an answer, or at least a compromise, and certain scriptural information also hints strongly at a conclusion. The deportation policy of the Assyrian Empire, for example, gives a clue as to where at least one portion of the ten tribes in general is located. And the Doctrine and Covenants, one of the standard works of the LDS Church, gives an important clue concerning the location of a second portion.

Because the Assyrians deported only one-half or less of a conquered city or region, bringing in foreign people from the outside as replacements, it follows that the one-half which remained in Palestine would eventually mix with incoming colonists and ultimately intermingle with people in other countries. This would identify the location of one portion of the ten tribes, those who were not taken into captivity but stayed in their original homeland, and at the same time partially verify the claim by some that the tribes are currently dispersed throughout the nations.

But the question of what happened to the captives in Assyria, at least those that banded together and disappeared into the north country, presents a more difficult problem, one where there appears to be no answer or solution without the intervention of a significant outside source of information. And in this case, it is the book known as the Doctrine and Covenants which once again presents a valuable clue. Only in this one source is there information indicating where the ten tribes might be located, in what manner they will return, and possibly how they disappeared from the land of Arzareth in the first place. In just a few verses of scripture, answers are given to a significant number of questions.

The name which appears on the book's title page is that of a man named Joseph Smith. He was not the author but rather the translator Prior to its publication, Joseph claimed to have received divine revelation on a large number of subjects, one of which pertained to the ten tribes of Israel. Eventually he published this material, and because of the way it originated, many people regarded him as a prophet and his revelations as scripture.

In relation to the tribes, especially how they will return someday, the Doctrine and Covenants gives new and important information. "And they who are in the north countries shall come in remembrance before the Lord," the record says, "and their prophets shall hear his voice, and shall no longer stay themselves; and they shall smite the rocks, and the ice shall flow down at their presence. And an highway shall be cast up in the midst of the great deep."[62]

Sometime in the future, a divine command will be given for the ten tribes to return. Prophets among them will "no longer stay themselves" or continue waiting for a signal to rejoin normal society, but will eventually make their way with their particular congregations to a place of exit. At this point, wherever it turns out to be, miraculous events will occur, much like the time when the Most High performed signs on the bank of the Euphrates River and Moses parted the waters of the Red Sea.

The prophets leading the people "will smite the rocks" at that time, apparently creating some type of aperture or opening through which the returning tribes will pass. A clue as to their general geographic location is given by reference to ice that will "flow down at their presence." It is then that a highway, or some kind of elevated passageway, will be raised up out of the sea in front of them in order for a potentially huge number of people to proceed further toward a destination.

In a scene that is again reminiscent of the children of Israel crossing the Red Sea, a throng of modern Israelites will traverse a large body of water, coming out of the north countries and heading toward the south, their objective being a new city called Zion, or the New Jerusalem, on the American Continent. There they will be welcomed by another group of Israelites, those specifically who are descendants of the tribe of Ephraim.

Whereas the ten tribes have a general ancestry from all of the tribes except Judah and possibly Levi, those awaiting them in Zion, according to the scripture, will be by direct lineage or adoption mainly from one particular tribe and will be called the "children of Ephraim." They are the ones who will not only welcome the returning tribes but will bestow upon them some type of glory, a spiritual gift or endowment. In return the tribes will bring with them gifts and treasures of their own.

"And they shall bring forth their rich treasures unto the children of Ephraim, my servants," states the scripture, "and the boundaries of the everlasting hills shall tremble at their presence. And there shall they fall down and be crowned with glory, even in Zion, by the hands of the servants of the Lord, even the children of Ephraim.

"And they shall be filled with songs of everlasting joy. Behold, this is the blessing of the everlasting God upon the tribes of Israel, and the richer blessing upon the head of Ephraim and his fellows."[63]

Surely these will be important events, involving unusual conditions and circumstances. Also it is significant that a description of the tribes returning in the future gives a clue and implication as to how they disappeared from the land of Arzareth in the past. The conditions of their disappearance, in other words, might well have been similar to those predicted for their return, including the features of rock, ice, and water, as well as an unusual highway or passageway.

But one thing appears certain, according to the account given in the Apocrypha, and that is that as the tribes originally began their journey from Assyria to Arzareth, there was a supernatural occurrence as they prepared to cross the Euphrates River. "For at that time the Most High performed signs for them and stopped the channels of the river until they had passed over."[64] From the beginning there were extraordinary circumstances, especially toward the end when they reached a preliminary destination and embarkation point. The implication is that it was here that they experienced a supernatural phenomenon that enabled them to enter a new area within the confines of the earth, conditions being comparable once again to those their descendants would encounter many centuries in the future.

In an isolated area in the north countries, therefore, somewhere in the land of the north so often referred to by the prophet Jeremiah, an extremely significant event took place. In the vicinity of the year 600 BC, soon after the destruction of Nineveh or possibly a short time earlier, that portion of the ten tribes who had resolved to "leave the multitude of the nations and go to a more distant region where mankind had never lived" now prepared to enter a new geographical area and lifetime. Their final destination was still unclear, yet their resolve to "keep their statutes which they had not kept in their own land" was always before them. And as they continued their journey, certainly they must have resembled in many ways the migration of the prophet Lehi, a much smaller group of Israelites yet one that was definitely contemporary and one also that was headed toward an unknown but promised land!

Chapter Eleven

Judah

Two groups of Israelites departed from the Middle East around the time of 600 BC, namely the family of Lehi in 597, according to modern chronology, and a group of Assyrian captives about the same time, who migrated into the north country. Two separate congregations of people, one small and the other undoubtedly much larger, both members of the house of Israel, left their homes for different reasons and departed into the wilderness. What they did was not something ill-conceived or incidental but enterprises well planned and carried out under the guidance of God himself.

Both migrations were part of a giant movement known as the Scattering of Israel. One by one, groups and members of the house of Israel were dispersed from the capital cities of Jerusalem and Samaria, as well as surrounding areas, and relocated to many different parts of the world.

"It appears that the house of Israel, sooner or later, will be scattered upon all the face of the earth," the scripture says, "and also among all nations. And behold, there are many who are already lost from the knowledge of those who are at Jerusalem. Yea, the more part of all the tribes have been led away, and they are scattered to and fro upon the isles of the sea; and whither they are none of us knoweth, save that we know that they have been led away."[65]

Among these Israelites there was still another group which left the Middle East in the area of 600 BC. Along with Lehi's party and those who banded together in Assyria, the people in a third congregation, again presumably small in number, left Judah's capital during its siege and downfall in the year 586 and commenced their own voyage to a promised land. Mulek, one of the sons of Zedekiah, in some way managed to escape his captors and with his own group departed from the stricken city of Jerusalem, most likely at night, and fled into the wilderness.

It is not known how many sons Zedekiah had, but evidently Nebuchadnezzar thought he had captured all of them, and he showed no mercy to what has been referred to as the royal seed. He promptly executed all of the boys in the presence of their father.

"Then they took the king, and carried him up unto the king of Babylon to Riblah in the land of Hamath, where he gave judgment upon him. And the king of Babylon slew the sons of Zedekiah before his eyes."[66]

But for whatever reason and purpose, there was one son who was able to escape. As with Lehi's group and those who disappeared into the north from Assyria, it was not his destiny, along with the ones who followed him, to be killed or enslaved by people such as the Chaldeans. Instead he departed from Jerusalem and traveled probably toward the west until he reached the seashore, at which place he built a ship, as Nephi was doing about the same time, and set sail with his small group of fugitives for the new world.

The similarities between Mulek's party, Lehi's party, and the ten tribes are no coincidence. All of these people had similar characteristics and purposes and disappeared from regular society around the same time. Certainly they lived in a unique period of history, a pivotal date in which highly significant events were taking place.

These three groups of Israelites especially are unique in that they ended up traveling to such distant places. Even those who departed from Assyria, whose ultimate destination and residence are still unknown, obviously journeyed to a place far removed from normal civilization and society

As for Mulek, according to the scripture, he and his group "were brought by the hand of the Lord across the great waters" where theoretically they landed at a location in the western hemisphere on the east coast, somewhere along the shoreline of the lower part of the Gulf of Mexico. In the record known as the Book of Mormon, it states that Mulek was brought into what became known as the land north or the land northward, whereas Lehi and his party apparently landed on the west coast, possibly somewhere in Central America, in what the Book of Mormon refers to as being in the land south or the land southward.[67]

The geography of Book of Mormon lands has long been a subject open to question, some scholars advocating a large-scale concept where North and Central America are the land northward and South America the land southward, with "a narrow neck of land" situated in between. Others regard the geography as being much more limited, interpreting part of southern Mexico as the land north and the other part along with upper Central America as the land south. The so-called narrow neck of land would then be the isthmus located by the Gulf of Tehuantepec.

It appears probable, therefore, that Mulek most likely landed on the east coast instead of the west, "it being the place of their first landing."[68] When the Chaldeans broke through the walls of Jerusalem, Zedekiah and his men fled eastward to the plains of Jericho but were soon overtaken, suggesting that escape in that direction was not feasible for others. The other direct route leading to a sea, most likely the Mediterranean, was westward, and theoretically that was where Mulek and his party went. Lehi and his group, on the other hand, built their ship in the southeastern part of the Arabian Peninsula and after crossing the Arabian Sea and the Indian and Pacific Oceans landed on the west coast, again at a location very possibly in Central America.

"Now the land south was called Lehi and the land north was called Mulek, which was after the son of Zedekiah; for the Lord did bring Mulek into the land north, and Lehi into the land south."[69]

Mulek and his people developed into a large civilization and after several centuries joined with other people who were descendants of Lehi. In the meantime, the latter had divided into two groups. Those who became known as Nephites followed Lehi's son Nephi, and the people called Lamanites were the descendants of Nephi's rebellious brothers, Laman and Lemuel. And so it was that Israelite people who had migrated from the city of Jerusalem around the time of 600 BC now existed as three significant populations in the new world, two who followed in the tradition of the prophet Lehi and the other who regarded the dissenting Laman as their ancestral leader!

Chapter Twelve

Israel

Sometime during the end of the seventh century BC and the beginning of the sixth, at least part of the ten tribes of Israel left their captivity site in Assyria and traveled to a region in the north country called Arzareth. It was there, as advocated by one view, that they mysteriously disappeared from among the nations and became known as the lost tribes. Yet another view states that following their arrival in the north, they eventually dispersed and intermingled with people in other countries, their descendants destined someday to be reassembled in a great process of gathering. Obviously the two opinions as stated are in opposition to one another, and one of the problems has to do with who it was among the ten tribes that was actually dispersed.

Because the Assyrians allegedly deported only one-half of a conquered population, and in some cases less, the portion that originally was *not taken* into captivity was consequently one which eventually was dispersed throughout the different countries. But the portion that was taken to various sections of the Assyrian Empire, as well as certain cities of the Medes, was a very separate and distinct group.

It was this group, in fact, or at least a certain percentage of it, that banded together and traveled further into the north country. Indeed it is this specific group of people, meaning their descendants, that modern scripture verifies as still being in existence, those who theoretically departed from the region of Arzareth during the period of 600 BC at a time contemporary with the departures of both Lehi and Mulek.

Yet whereas the general locality of Lehi and Mulek has been confirmed, no definite information exists on the whereabouts of the lost tribes, only that they were last seen or accounted for in the north country. No other information is available except the account which is found in the Apocrypha. The only possible clue as to where the tribes might be presently located is found in a brief passage of scripture where the conditions and circumstances of their future return imply the type of place to which they were taken after reaching the land of Arzareth.

"And they who are in the north countries shall come in remembrance before the Lord," the scripture says, "and their prophets shall hear his voice, and shall no longer stay themselves; and they shall smite the rocks, and the ice shall flow down at their presence. And an highway shall be cast up in the midst of the great deep."[70]

This scripture strongly suggests that the lost tribes were originally taken to a remote and unorthodox site somewhere in the north country and from there relocated to another region or locality. In no other way can the mysterious disappearance of this group of people be explained except to say that by miraculous and supernatural circumstances they were separated from regular society by God himself and removed to a new area, not on the actual surface of the earth, which has been thoroughly mapped and explored, but to some other place within its confines.

This is not to say that the tribes traveled to some exotic destination like the center of the earth or a location unreasonably far beneath its surface. But the scriptures do suggest that they were taken somewhere else within the earth's structure and organization, whether it be at a physical level or one that is spiritual.

The spirit world, for example, according to the theology of the

Mormon Church, by way of some unknown phenomenon is said to be on the earth itself, not on its visible surface but in a region nevertheless within its spiritual makeup or organization. In some way, the earth is able to serve a dual purpose.

Consequently, it is possible to visualize some type of existence in which the earth might accommodate the lost tribes of Israel. This in turn suggests that the tribes are currently hidden in some geographical area that is unmapped and unexplored, a concept that is unorthodox but still a possibility. To accept it, however, is understandably difficult, and a natural inclination at first is to reject it and look for other explanations.

A well-known scientist and theologian on one occasion, while speaking to a Mormon congregation, cautioned people against this kind of rationalization. His name was James E. Talmage. "There is a tendency among men," he said, "to explain away what they do not wish to understand in literal simplicity, and we as Latter-day Saints are not entirely free from the taint of that tendency."

At the time, Dr. Talmage was talking about the lost tribes, referring specifically to the prediction that someday they would return in an unusual manner. "Some people say that prediction is to be explained in this way," he continued. "A gathering is in progress, and has been in progress from the early days of this church, and thus the 'lost tribes' are now being gathered but that we are not to look for the return of any body of people now unknown as to their whereabouts.

"True, the gathering is in progress," he said. "This is a gathering dispensation. But the prophecy stands that the tribes shall be brought forth from their hiding place, bringing their scriptures with them."[71]

In regard to the earth itself, it must be said that it is a very unusual place and much more than just a planet in the solar system. From a scientific standpoint, it is an astronomical body that is composed of an inner and outer core, along with a mantle and crust, yet at the same time scriptural accounts suggest that it has an extremely unusual potential and is more than its geological features imply.

The earth, in fact, might be considered a living organism, even to the extent of possessing a soul. Just as the spirit and body constitute the soul of a man, so might the combined spiritual and temporal parts of the planet be regarded as the soul of the earth. Such a concept recognizes the earth's true identity and avoids the error of classifying it merely as a geological or astronomical sphere.

In view of this, certainly it is a possibility that the people known as the lost tribes of Israel are still somewhere within the earth's confines, not dispersed throughout the world's population or located mainly in the north country but at a more unorthodox and remote location known only to God himself. He is the one who led them there in the beginning, and according to the scriptural account in the Doctrine and Covenants, he is the one who will initiate their return. In the meantime, it is a matter of people having faith, as well as intellect, believing that a divine purpose is involved and anticipating the approach of future events.

And on some historic occasion, at a time not too far away, when crumbling rock and ice have opened up a passageway in the north countries and a mysterious highway has appeared, people will then know that the ten tribes of Israel are finally on their way, traveling together as a great multitude and coming from a place where they have been hidden for centuries after disappearing from the land of Arzareth in the time of 600 BC!

Chapter Thirteen

Assyria

At the time that Lehi and his small group departed from Jerusalem, the Assyrian Empire in the north had recently just come to an end. The capital city of Ninevah was conquered and destroyed in 612 BC, and in its wake were just a few years of resistance before the once mighty empire, so long feared by surrounding nations, finally fell. For the family of Lehi and many others, it must have been a time of emotion and uncertainty, all wondering what the immediate future might bring.

It was undoubtedly difficult for people to visualize what it had been like when Assyria was not the ruling nation. This one country had been a significant force in the Middle East for centuries, and during the zenith of its power in approximately 750–625 BC, the time of its most famous kings, it built the largest empire the world had ever seen. Hated and feared, and yet respected for its overwhelming superiority, there was a long period of history when it seemed to be invincible

As far as the Israelites were concerned, Assyria became a critically important factor in about 733 BC when Tiglath-Pileser III invaded the Kingdom of Israel, entering northern Palestine and areas east of the Jordan River and subjugating a large number of cities. Nine years later another king, Shalmaneser V, attacked the capital city of Samaria in central Palestine, and after a three-year siege both the city and entire kingdom succumbed to the Assyrians, most likely to Sargon II, who recently had become the new ruler. In the meantime the Kingdom of Judah to the south fortunately escaped similar devastation. Its demise would not occur for another century or more, at a time when Assyria itself had been defeated.

Two decades prior to Lehi's departure from Jerusalem, the Assyrian Empire was already struggling for survival. The era of its most successful kings had passed, and for a time the new and inexperienced rulers attempted to keep the empire intact. The last important king had been Ashurbanipal, who ruled for forty years, but those who followed merely became witnesses to a royal kingdom and empire falling apart.

Even during the reign of Ashurbanipal there had been signs that Assyria was in trouble: the declining industries and agriculture, an increasing intervention in commerce and trade by outside influence, and a disintegration within the military, where more and more foreigners were incorporated into the armed forces. A significant example of the latter is that of certain Israelite captives who were deported from Samaria.

When Sargon II conquered the Kingdom of Israel, part of the booty taken was 200 chariots, and presumably those who drove them, all of which was conscripted into the military. According to government records, these men became a well-known cohort in the Assyrian cavalry and were led by a commanding officer and fifteen subordinate commanders, most of whom were allegedly Semitic in origin. Undoubtedly there were many other such instances, and whereas the policy of including foreigners in the military initially seemed to be a good idea, as did accepting foreign influence in other areas, it eventually became a serious problem. Definitely it was a contributing factor during the year 612 BC as the invading armies of the people known as the Medes and Chaldeans attacked the city of Nineveh and completely destroyed Assyria's capital. The Assyrian king at this time was

Sin-shar-ishkun, a son of Ashurbanipal.

Sin-shar-ishkun had been the undisputed sovereign of Assyria for more than a decade, terminating a period of political insecurity and unrest, but now that his reign was coming to an end he allegedly took his own life. Although there was no sure evidence of what actually happened, both tradition and circumstances suggest that the king set fire to himself and his possessions in a giant funeral pyre.

Certainly it was an ignominious way for any person of royalty to die. The king's father had reigned forty years, enjoying in many ways an illustrious career, but now his unfortunate son perished in a fiery blaze, if not one of his own making then surely one enjoined upon him by the destroying invaders who enveloped his city in fire. And in a very short time, it was not only a king and a city that died but also an empire, one that had long been a tyrant and despot among the nations.

As Nineveh fell that day to the Medes and Chaldeans, and possibly people known as the Scythians, there was an echo, as it were, of the misery and woe inflicted by forces of the Assyrian Empire. In the words of Nahum, a prophet in the Bible, scenes and images of invading Assyrian armies were brought to a vivid remembrance. "The chariots shall rage in the streets," he said. "They shall justle one against another in the broad ways: they shall seem like torches, they shall run like the lightnings."

Then in specific reference to Nineveh, he condemned the city for its wickedness and brutality and predicted its defeat and downfall. "Woe to the bloody city!" he cried. "It is all full of lies and robbery; the prey departeth not; the noise of a whip, and the noise of the rattling of the wheels, and of the prancing horses, and of the jumping chariots. The horseman lifteth up both the bright sword and the glittering spear: and there is a multitude of slain, and a great number of carcases; and there is none end of their corpses," Nahum lamented.

"Behold, I am against thee, saith the Lord of hosts; and I will discover thy skirts upon thy face, and I will shew the nations thy nakedness, and the kingdoms thy shame. And it shall come to pass, that all they that look upon thee, shall flee from thee and say, Nineveh is laid waste: who will bemoan her? whence shall I seek comforters for thee?

"Thy shepherds slumber," the prophet concluded. "O king of Assyria: thy nobles shall dwell in the dust: thy people is scattered upon the mountains, and no man gathereth them. There is no healing of thy bruise; thy wound is grievous: all that hear the bruit of thee shall clap the hands over thee: for upon whom hath not thy wickedness passed continually?"[72]

For so many years the city of Nineveh had been the symbol of a mighty empire. Situated on the banks of the Tigris River, it was the place where the prophet Jonah traveled after being cast from the belly of a whale and also the capital and royal residence of some of the most well-known Assyrian kings, including Sennacherib, Essarhaddon, and Ashurbanipal. All of its history and fame quickly began to fade, however, as news spread throughout the Middle East that Nineveh had been conquered and destroyed. Regardless of who the victors were, who might now become as ruthless and notorious as their predecessors, it was still significant that a perennial threat was finally gone. A new milestone had been reached and with it also a new hope for the future.

And among all those who heard of Assyria's fall, at a place several hundred miles from where it happened, there was one specific group of people who were undoubtedly apprehensive of what had happened and indeed still very much unaware of what lay ahead for them, namely the prophet Lehi and members of his family, citizens of the Kingdom of Judah who were residing somewhere in the suburbs of Jerusalem!

Chapter Fourteen

Assyria

News reports coming into Jerusalem, as well as other important centers of the Middle East, undoubtedly gave the impression that the Assyrian Empire had come to an end. The city of Ashur, a former capital, had fallen to Median armies in 614 BC, and now two years later in 612, as Nineveh itself lay in ruins and was burning, it definitely appeared that all resistance had ended. The king Sin-shar-ishkun had perished in flames, and with no one in the royal line to succeed him, both the Medes and Chaldeans apparently ruled supreme.

But what no one knew at the time was that part of the Assyrian army had broken through the invaders and escaped to the city of Harren west of Nineveh. There they regrouped, and in the face of all that had happened, and despite the overwhelming power and threat of Media and Chaldea, and possibly the Scythians, a certain figure stepped forward and took charge, declaring himself to be the king of Assyria.

He might have been one of Sin-shar-ishkun's nobles, the turtan or provisional governor of Harran, although in actuality his true identity will probably always be in question. Harran was considered to be a "western capital of the empire," being in a strategic location in regard to places such as Syria and Egypt and areas along the Mediterranean, and one such as the turtan or "commander in chief" in that region, the officer next in dignity to the king himself, would certainly be a logical person to come forth at this time and assume command.

His name was Ashur-uballit II, someone heretofore unknown in history, yet one who now accepted the challenge of trying to save Assyria, making the attempt in the face of almost impossible odds to rescue a dying nation. He was the namesake of a famous king named Ashur-uballit I who preceded him by several centuries and ruled Assyria for three decades in the middle of the fourteenth century BC His distant predecessor had won independence for his people at that time and raised the nation to be a significant power in the Middle East.

Now a new ruler in a different setting faced the task of rebuilding a war-torn country and elevating it once again to its former status among the nations, at the same time stemming the tide of invading armies coming from the north and east. His only hope in doing this was to receive help from the nearby forces of Egypt who pledged assistance coming from the south.

Egypt had been aiding Assyria as far back as 616 BC, two years before the conquest of Ashur. Its motive undoubtedly was to assist its neighbor in resisting the threatening raids of the Medes, Chaldeans, and Scythians. Certainly it was to Egypt's advantage to keep Assyria as a buffer zone between itself and the invaders. In this situation, therefore, Ashur-uballit and his army, along with whatever reinforcements he received from Egypt, barricaded themselves in the stronghold of Harran and waited for an imminent invasion.

Harran was an important city located on the Balikh River, a tributary of the Euphrates. It was a historic area, having been the place where Abraham and his party traveled after leaving Ur of the Chaldees. It was also the area where Abraham's servant later went to find a wife for Isaac and where Jacob fled to get away from his brother Esau. From this place all but one of the twelve tribes of Israel originated. Moreover, it might well have been one of several cities where Israelite captives were eventually deported from Palestine and Transjordan.

Aside from its biblical significance, however, Harran was also known for its strategic location on important roads and trade routes in the Middle East. Situated at an intersection between Nineveh, Carchemish, Damascus, and Egypt, it had long been an important political and commercial center. Its location was especially conducive to interaction with Egypt.

Of particular importance also was the fact that Harran was a well-known religious center. It was here that a temple of the moon-god Sin was located; a second temple was in Ur to the southeast. At the sanctuaries of Ehulhul in Harran and Egissirgal in Ur, religious ceremonies were performed. Ashurbanipal, the last important Assyrian king, was himself interested in the moon worship which took place at the Ehulhul shrine.

Indeed, all of this provides an interesting and significant background to the city of Harran, a city that was now attacked in 610 BC by the forces of Media and Chaldea, eventually forcing Ashur-uballit and his allies to abandon their position and flee toward the south across the Euphrates River. In the meantime, the invaders reduced Harren to ruins and plundered the sanctuary of Ehulhul and its temple.

It is uncertain why Egypt did not give more assistance to Assyria in the defense of Harren. But whatever the reason for delay, additional help did arrive the following year. It was about this time that a new pharaoh came on the scene, and for several years Egypt became more involved.

During the year 609 BC the Assyrians and Egyptians crossed back over the Euphrates River and attempted to regain Harran. They made several assaults upon the city without success and then withdrew after a two-month siege when a Chaldean army suddenly appeared.

In the following year the pharaoh known as Necho II came to the battle area in person. While traveling through Palestine, where he was opposed by Josiah, king of Judah, he reluctantly killed the king and then continued on to Assyria, spending the next several years fighting along with the Assyrians against the Medes and especially the Chaldeans. During this time Ashur-uballit apparently was still in command of his army and had no intention of giving up. As long as Egypt was involved, particularly under its new leadership, he seemed optimistic that something still might happen which would be to his advantage. This was his hope and dream, and with the memory of a former king and predecessor in mind, of whom he was a namesake, he continued to oppose the aggressor for three more years.

Sin-shar-ishkun had died in the fire at Nineveh, but another king had taken his place and was now determined to persevere to the end. And that end finally came in 605 BC in the city of Carchemish, on the banks of the Euphrates River, about sixty miles west of Harren!

CHAPTER FIFTEEN

Assyria

IT WAS IN CARCHEMISH that the Egyptians and Assyrians made one last stand against the forces of Chaldea. The Chaldean king at this time had transferred the control of his army to his son, the crown prince Nebuchadnezzar, and it was he who now descended upon the unfortunate city on the Euphrates, attacking from the north as well as the south. The invaders were well prepared to make a final assault, and as Necho and his forces waited, along with Ashur-uballit and what was left of his army, it was a dramatic and crucial moment.

Certainly much was at stake, not only for the Egyptians and Assyrians, but others as well. The Greeks north of the Mediterranean, for example, who were concerned and interested in the political situation in the Middle East, allegedly sent mercenary soldiers in time to participate in the battle at Carchemish, their purpose being to help counter the threat posed by the aggressions of Chaldea, Media, and Scythia. Again it was with the idea of keeping Assyria as a bulwark and buffer against the invading people that they supported the army.

But it was all to no avail as Nebuchadnezzar and his Chaldean forces were overwhelmingly victorious. The fierce battle which took place on the banks of the Euphrates River reduced the city of Carchemish to a mass of blazing ruins. Any hope of Assyria remaining intact as a nation now completely disappeared as all vestiges of an empire came to an end.

Along with anything else that might be said about this important event, by any historian or commentator, the brief account in the Bible is as descriptive and significant as any. Appropriately it is given by the prophet Jeremiah shortly after the battle happened.

"The word of the Lord which came to Jeremiah the prophet against the Gentiles, against Egypt, against the army of Pharaoh-necho king of Egypt, which was by the river Euphrates in Carchemish, which Nebuchadnezzar king of Babylon smote in the fourth year of Jehoiakim the son of Josiah king of Judah. Order ye the buckler and shield, and draw near to battle. Harness the horses; and get up, ye horsemen, and stand forth with your helmets; furbish the spears, and put on the brigandines."[73]

"Who is this that cometh up as a flood, whose waters are moved as the rivers? Egypt risest up like a flood, and his waters are moved like the rivers; and he saith, I will go up, and will cover the earth; I will destroy the city and the inhabitants thereof."[74]

"This is the day of the Lord God of hosts," Jeremiah continued, "a day of vengeance, that he may avenge him of his adversaries: and the sword shall devour, and it shall be satiate and made drunk with their blood: for the Lord God of hosts hath a sacrifice in the north country by the river Euphrates."[75]

It is unknown whether or not Necho and Ashur-uballit were actually in Carchemish at the time of the invasion. Nebuchadnezzar might well have been present, but the Egyptian and Assyrian leaders possibly were elsewhere. In any case, it was not uncommon for heads of state to direct military operations from a separate location, especially at places such as the city of Riblah in the south.

In any case, the defenders of Carchemish were soundly defeated and the survivors scattered from the city. The Egyptian forces retreated to the area in Syria called Hamath where they allegedly were annihilated. Other reports state that Nebuchadnezzar pursued them as far as the Egyptian border and stopped only when he learned that his father had died in Chaldea, causing him to secure an understanding and commitment from Necho and return home.

As for Ashur-uballit, his outcome and destiny will always remain a mystery. One story has it that he continued resistance in the regions near Urartu, north of Assyria, and yet another possibility is that he stayed with his army to the end and perished in the holocaust at Carchemish. Surely his dream concerning Assyria was a noble one, but it never materialized, and with his possible death the plans for beginning a new Assyrian Empire died also!

Chapter Sixteen

Chaldea

The Medes and the Chaldeans who conquered Assyria came from geographical areas occupied respectively by modern-day Iran and Iraq. In regard to the latter, the people were descendants of tribes known as the Kaldu, hence the name of Chaldea.

In the middle of the seventh century BC, the Chaldeans were a highly significant group in Babylonia. It was in this region that the well-known Ur of the Chaldees was located as well as Babylon, one possible site of the Tower of Babel. Situated between the lower stretches of the Tigris and Euphrates Rivers, the land was the scene of many important events in history.

This was especially true in the time of Lehi the prophet. The time preceding 600 BC, as well as immediately after, was characterized by many dramatic occurrences that had a tremendous impact on the lives of people living in the Middle East. During this specific time period, many faced uncertain futures, including those who lived in Chaldea.

In the year 625, a man named Nabopolassar was a Chaldean governor in the Assyrian Empire. He served as viceroy of the Sealands, the large area of marshes in southern Babylonia. He had been an important official during the reign of Ashurbanipal, but as a new king came into power, he suddenly rebelled and declared his country's independence, referring to himself as the king of Babylon. It was the beginning of a new era in the history of Mesopotamia, and in the years that followed, Nabopolassar organized an army and challenged the authority of Assyria, subjugating cities and territory in Babylonia and eventually setting his sights on the capital city of Nineveh.

In 616 BC he entered Assyria proper, moving up the Euphrates River as far as Harran and along the Tigris to the strategic city of Ashur, an important religious center and former capital. He decided to attack Ashur two years later but upon arriving found that it had already been conquered by the Medes, a people who themselves had recently declared their independence from Assyria. The Median king at this time was Cyaxares, who welcomed Nabopolassar as a friend and ally in planning a future attack on Nineveh.

The alliance made by the two men amid the ruins of Ashur was ratified by a marital contract between royal siblings. It was arranged that Nebuchadnezzar, the crown prince of Chaldea, would marry the Median princess Amytis. One report says that she was the daughter of Cyaxares, yet another that she was his granddaughter, the daughter of his son and future successor Astyages. In any case, the agreement was made between the two rulers, and the fate of Nineveh was sealed.

The city's downfall in 612 BC included a two-month siege, followed by a complete desolation and burning. Unlike Ashur further down the river, the capital was reduced to a veritable mound of ashes. Chaldeans and Medes, and allegedly also the Scythians, inflicted a total destruction upon the city, although the main force of attack was apparently carried out by the Medes. There are indications, in fact, that it was the Median armies who were mainly responsible for military victories occurring during these years. Indeed, their ferocity and intensity of battle were much like that of the Assyrians.

Two years later, when the Medes and Chaldeans attacked Harran west of Nineveh, it was Media once again who did most of the fighting. It was they also who destroyed the famous Temple of Sin, the well-known center of moon worship in the city.

The story is that Nabopolassar was not in favor of destroying the temple, and instead of sleeping in his own bed that night he slept on an earthen floor, in biblical essence a symbol of putting on sackcloth and ashes. The Chaldean king, like Ashurbanipal of Assyria before him, had a deep respect for the Harran temple and regretted its desecration.

During the time that followed, the Assyrians, with the help of Egypt, made one last attempt to save an empire. Led by a self-proclaimed king named Ashur-uballit, and by the Egyptian pharaoh Necho II, two nations who earlier had opposed one another now attempted unsuccessfully to regain Harren. They spent the next four years fighting against Nabopolassar and the Chaldeans. It was a valiant but futile effort to prevent a final conquest. All of this accompanied the eclipse and disintegration of what had been a powerful empire and was prelude to the departure of the prophet Lehi and his family from Jerusalem!

Chapter Seventeen

Chaldea

At the time that Nineveh was destroyed, many in the Middle East exulted that the long reign of a tyrant nation was nearing an end. After a long period of military aggression and conquest by a people known for its intimidation and brutality, the world was soon to be free from a power that had been universally feared. And among all the voices of jubilation concerning Nineveh, none were more poignant than those of the prophets Nahum and Zepheniah in the Kingdom of Judah.

"But Nineveh is of old like a pool of water," said Nahum, "yet they shall flee away. Stand, stand, shall they cry; but none shall look back . . . She is empty, and void, and waste: and the heart melteth, and the knees smite together, and much pain is in all loins, and the faces of them all gather blackness . . . Behold, I am against thee, saith the Lord of hosts, and I will burn her chariots in the smoke, and the sword shall devour thy young lions; and I will cut off thy prey from the earth, and the voice of thy messengers shall no more be heard."[76]

And concerning the Lord and his dire forecast for the city, Zephaniah said, "And he will stretch out his hand against the north, and destroy Assyria; and will make Nineveh a desolation, and dry like a wilderness. And flocks shall lie down in the midst of her, all the beasts of the nations; both the cormorant and the bittern shall lodge in the upper lintels of it; their voice shall sing in the windows; desolation shall be in the thresholds: for he shall uncover the cedar work.

"This is the rejoicing city that dwelt carelessly," he continued, "that said in her heart, I am, and there is none beside me: how is she become a desolation, a place for beasts to lie down in; every one that passeth by her shall hiss, and wag his hand."[77]

After the fall of Nineveh, however, and before Assyria's final death knell sounded, one final step had to be taken by the Chaldeans, namely the conquest and destruction of the city of Carchemish. In successive campaigns against Ashur and Nineveh, and later against Harran, most of the opposition had been removed, and only the stronghold of Carchemish remained. The last vestiges of the Assyrian military, along with the forces of Egypt and also Greek mercenaries, were stationed there and prepared to fight. Presumably the Assyrians were still led by the valiant Ashur-uballit, yet even with the support of an Egyptian pharaoh, there was little question about the outcome of battle, and the end of Assyria seemed inevitable.

In 605 BC, therefore, being five years prior to Lehi's departure from Jerusalem, or eight years according to Book of Mormon chronology, Carchemish fell to the Chaldeans. This time it was not a Median or Scythian victory but one mainly executed by Chaldea.

Nor was it Nabopolassar who directed the last invasion. In the final onslaught it was the crown prince Nebuchadnezzar who commanded the Chaldean army. He was the one who defeated Carchemish and then pursued the enemy deep into Syrian territory. The fate of Ashur-uballit is unknown, but the Egyptian pharaoh escaped, although much of his army, if not all of it, was annihilated.

According to one account, the Egyptian forces were destroyed en masse by the Chaldeans in the Syrian city of Hamath. Another says that Nebuchadnezzar followed the survivors to the Egyptian border, stopping only when he learned of his father's death in Babylonia, which necessitated his return home to be crowned the new king of Chaldea.

It was also at this time, soon after his victory at Carchemish, that he entered the city of Jerusalem in the Kingdom of Judah, exacting allegiance and tribute from the king and confiscating treasure and booty from the temple. In addition, he took a certain number of people into captivity, including Daniel and his friends Shadrach, Meshach, and Abednego, thus initiating what came to be known as the Babylonian Captivity.

"In the third year of the reign of Jehoiakim king of Judah came Nebuchadnezzar king of Babylon unto Jerusalem, and besieged it. And the Lord gave Jehoiakim king of Judah into his hand, with part of the vessels of the house of God: which he carried into the land of Shinar to the house of his god; and he brought the vessels into the treasure house of his god."[78]

This time period was especially important, not just because it relates to the prophet Lehi but also because it marks the beginning of the reign of Nebuchadnezzar, one of the most colorful figures in both secular and biblical history. Similar to the reign of Ashurbanipal in Assyria, he ruled in Chaldea for 42 years, excelling as an administrator both culturally and economically, as well as politically and in the military. In the Bible especially he is noted for his conquests of Jerusalem and the unusual association he had with the prophet Daniel.

During Nebuchadnezzar's second year as king, according to the biblical record, it being two or three years following the Battle of Carchemish, he saw a great image in a dream which Daniel was able to interpret. Magicians, astrologers, and sorcerers failed to find any interpretation, but the secret of the dream was revealed to Daniel in a night vision

"Thou, O king, sawest, and behold a great image," he told Nebuchadnezzar. "This great image, whose brightness was excellent, stood before thee; and the form thereof was terrible."[79]

Daniel then described the image as having a head of fine gold, breast and arms of silver, and stomach and thighs made of brass. Its legs were of iron, he said, and its feet part iron and part clay.

He also told the king about a certain stone cut out of a mountain without hands, a stone that broke the image and all of its parts into pieces. These were then reduced to chaff like grain on a threshing floor and carried away in the wind. Finally the stone became a great mountain and filled the whole earth.

Nebuchadnezzar was informed that he himself was the image's head of gold and that the other parts were symbolic of future kingdoms. "Thou, O king, art a king of kings," Daniel told him, "for the God of heaven hath given thee a kingdom, and power, and strength, and glory." But eventually, he said, all kingdoms would pass away.[80]

The historicity of the book of Daniel in the Bible has often been questioned, especially in regard to the person of Nebuchadnezzar. But the king's reaction to Daniel's interpretation of his dream is nevertheless interesting.

"Then the king Nebuchadnezzar fell upon his face, and worshipped Daniel," the record says, "and commanded that they should offer an oblation and sweet odors unto him… Of a truth it is, that your God is a God of gods," he said, "and a Lord of kings, and a revealer of secrets, seeing thou couldest reveal this secret."[81]

The king gave Daniel many gifts and made him a ruler in the province of Babylon, naming him the chief of governors over all of the wise men. At Daniel's request, similar authority was also granted to his three friends Shadrach, Meshach, and Abednego. But it was Daniel's specific station to sit in the gate of the king.

It is interesting to compare Nebuchadnezzar as a crown prince in the Battle of Carchemish with the same person as a Chaldean monarch in Babylon a few years later, observing the acts and statements attributed to him by the Bible. Again it is another instance that requires faith as well as intellect in arriving at the truth of a matter, much like visualizing Jonah in the belly of a whale on his way to Nineveh. And the things which eventually happened to Daniel's three friends during this same time period are no less challenging.

Sometime after the interpretation of Nebuchadnezzar's dream, the king constructed a huge image or statue of gold and set it in what was called the plain of Dura in Babylon. In seeming contradiction to what he had said earlier, he then commanded all of the people to fall down and worship the golden image, the penalty for disobedience being condemnation to death in a burning fiery furnace. The people obeyed, of course, but it was soon brought to the king's attention that certain Jews who occupied important positions in the city, namely Shadrach, Meshach, and Abednego, did not cooperate.

In a rage of anger, the king had the men brought before him, and when they said they would not worship any image or serve Chaldean gods, he condemned them to be burned in the furnace. "Then was Nebuchadnezzar full of fury, and the form of his visage was changed against Shadrach, Meshach, and Abednego; therefore he spake, and commanded that they should heat the furnace one seven times more than it was wont to be heated. And he commanded the most mighty men that were in his army to bind Shadrach, Meshach, and Abednego, and to cast them into the burning fiery furnace."[82]

In the presence of the king and his counselors, Daniel's friends were immediately bound and thrown into the flames. Also witnessing the event were the king's princes and governors, along with certain captains of the military. It was an impressive occasion for them, and the furnace had been fired so intensely that the flames even consumed the men carrying out the execution. But by some kind of miracle, the three Israelites survived and could be seen alive in the fire.

Nebuchadnezzar was astonished and in haste turned to his counselors and said, "Did not we cast three men bound into the midst of the fire? They answered and said unto the king, True, O king. He answered and said, Lo, I see four men loose, walking in the midst of the fire, and they have no hurt; and the form of the fourth is like the Son of God."

Then the king called to Daniel's friends and told them to come out of the furnace, noting that the fire had not harmed them, "nor was an hair of their head singed, neither were their coats changed, nor the smell of fire had passed on them . . . Blessed be the God of Shadrach, Meshach, and Abednego," Nebuchadnezzar said, "who hath sent his angel, and delivered his servants that trusted in him and have changed the king's word, and yielded their bodies, that they might not serve nor worship any god, except their own God.

"Therefore I make a decree," he proclaimed, "that every people, nation, and language, which speak any thing amiss against the God of Shadrach, Meshach, and Abednego, shall be cut in pieces, and their houses shall be made a dunghill: because there is no other God that can deliver after this sort."[83]

As to the reality of someone like Nebuchadnezzar reacting in this manner, along with his alleged actions when earlier he "fell upon his face and worshipped Daniel," the words of Jeremiah at one time give the idea that the Chaldean king was more than the ordinary Middle Eastern monarch and was maybe capable, for a time at least, of acting as he did. In speaking to the rulers of Edom, Moab, and Ammon, for example, as well as to Tyre and Sidon, he quoted the Lord by saying, "And now have I given all these lands into the hand of Nebuchadnezzar the king of Babylon, my servant; and the beasts of the field have I given him also to serve him. And all nations shall serve him, and his son, and his son's son, until the very time of his land come: and then many nations and great kings shall serve themselves of him."[84]

Indeed it was a unique time in history, if the words of the Bible are correct, when a man of such stature was accorded this kind of recognition by Deity. It was a time when God himself referred to Nebuchadnezzar as his servant. And yet it was only temporary, for in the words of Jeremiah it was made known that the Chaldean king would eventually be punished for what he had done to Israel and the surrounding nations, and that Babylon in Chaldea would "become heaps, a dwellingplace for dragons, an astonishment, and an hissing, without an inhabitant."[85] Certainly it was an interesting period of time when unusual circumstances and events were coinciding and coming together!

Chapter Eighteen

Chaldea

According to the book of Daniel, it was in the second year of Nebuchadnezzar's reign that the king had his dream of the golden image. This was approximately 603 BC by way of the present calendar, or three years earlier in 606 according to the Book of Mormon. The incident pertaining to Daniel's three friends in the fiery furnace, therefore, might have occurred only a short time before Lehi left Jerusalem. It was also at this time that the Chaldean king was approaching the climax of his career.

Nineveh had ceased to exist, but the city of Babylon increased in size and importance to where it was now regarded as a metropolitan center of the Middle East. Whereas the capital of Assyria had been the focal point of commerce and politics for so many years, it was now the Chaldean capital which became a focus of attention in the ancient world. In and around Mesopotamia the city was a strategic intersection for merchants and travelers coming in from all directions.

This particular area was a locality that might well have been visited by Lehi, who is reputed to have been a merchant who traveled great distances. It is possible that his business ventures took him toward the south to places along the Arabian Peninsula and to Egyptian cities like Memphis and even Thebes. Also to the north were the important cities of Nineveh and Babylon, as well as commercial areas north of the Mediterranean such as Athens and Corinth in Greece. Too much should not be attributed to Lehi's potential for travel during his possible career as a merchant, yet on the other hand neither should it be underestimated.

It is known now more then ever before in the modern era that the ancient world of travel was not the scene of occasional caravans and small groups of nomads but rather one characterized by a large host of merchants and other such travelers who covered amazing distances, especially considering their available means of transportation. This would consequently be true of Lehi the prophet, who not only pursued a professional career as a merchant, but also may have traveled as a "tourist," encountering many different regions and cultures.

A visit to northern Mesopotamia during this time period, for example, prior to the demise of Assyria, would reveal two important cities, one the Assyrian capital and the other a short distance away that was a former capital. In the reign of Sargon II (721–705 BC), the king built a new city and seat of government a few miles northeast of Nineveh which he named Dur-Sharrukin, also called Sargonsburg. It was ten years in construction and was built by engineers and workmen from Assyria in addition to captive people imported from outside areas. Sargon himself said that he built Dur-Sharrukin mostly with the labor of foreign people, among whom were members of the ten tribes of Israel including some taken from Samaria.

This city was no longer the capital in Lehi's day, it having been replaced by Sennacherib (704–681), who established a new capital at Nineveh. But it did exist as an important site in the Assyrian Empire and was undoubtedly still impressive as a city with a numerous population and former government buildings and palaces.

In its place Nineveh became the center place and showpiece of the ancient world. During the administrations of Sennacherib, Esarhaddon (680–669), and Ashurbanipal (668–627), the last of the great kings or emperors, and also the few rulers that followed them (626–605), it was the epitome of culture and progress, as well as a powerful yet somber symbol of aggression and authority. Surely it was a city to be respected and also feared, and especially for people coming in from the outside, a visit would undoubtedly be impressive.

Sennacherib expanded and beautified Nineveh by erecting expensive palaces and temples and also fortifying the city walls. Situated on the Tigris River, it was encircled by a massive wall two-and-a-half miles long and eight miles in total circumference. In Lehi's time the city comprised a population of possibly 300,000 people, much larger than in the time of Jonah a century and a half earlier.

Jonah, of course, had been commanded to go to Nineveh. "Arise, go to Nineveh, that great city," the Lord told him on one occasion, "and cry against it; for their wickedness is come up before me." But Jonah procrastinated, and his roundabout journey took him through the body of a whale. At that time the Lord spoke to him again.

"And the word of the Lord came unto Jonah the second time, saying, Arise, go unto Nineveh, that great city, and preach unto it the preaching that I bid thee. So Jonah arose, and went unto Nineveh, according to the word of the Lord. Now Nineveh was an exceeding great city of three days journey. And Jonah began to enter into the city a day's journey, and he cried, and said, Yet forty days, and Nineveh shall be overthrown."

The story of what happened to the city on that occasion is well known. It was spared because of its alleged repentance, and Jonah was unhappy because of how things turned out. "And should I not spare Nineveh, that great city," the Lord asked the prophet, "wherein are more than sixscore thousand persons that cannot discern between their right hand and their left hand, and also much cattle?"[86]

It is interesting in this account that two important pieces of information are given: the amount of time it took Jonah to go from his starting point to the city, namely three days, and the number of people living there at the time, which was six score thousand or 120,000. A trip taken later by Lehi via camel would undoubtedly have taken considerably longer.

In addition to Nineveh, Lehi's business trips also could have taken him to Babylon. Although the city was completely destroyed by Sennacherib, it was rebuilt by his successor, Esarhaddon, and by Middle Eastern standards in the time of Lehi it was a prominent and flourishing metropolis. Nabopolassar and Nebuchadnezzar especially were responsible for making the capital not only a showpiece of architectural and artistic grandeur but a hub of commercial and political activity.

A visit to the city, particularly during the time of Nebuchadnezzar, would have presented the viewer with an impressive scene, and upon leaving one would say he had witnessed something far beyond the ordinary. Much like Nineveh and Dur-sharrukin, which had excelled in previous years, Babylon by the end of the seventh century BC was a new creation, the product of two master builders, father and son, the co-founders of the nation of Chaldea and the so-called Neo-Babylonian Empire. The city was indeed a glistening jewel situated between two rivers.

The main entrance to Babylon was in the northern sector at what was known as the Gate of Ishtar. This consisted of a double archway with two large towers on each side, rising as high as thirty-four feet. Originally colored blue, the giant towers were adorned with more than 500 bull and dragon reliefs in contrasting color. Their remains are still standing today and were once regarded as the most impressive sight in Babylon, a view that centuries ago might well have greeted incoming captives from Judah during the Babylonian Captivity.

Entrance through the Ishtar Gate marked the beginning of a long avenue or thoroughfare called Procession Street. Enclosed by walls twenty feet high, it was the Sacred Way in the city, not a street accommodating daily traffic but one used by worshipers going to a temple complex in order to pay homage to the Chaldean god Marduk. On the way was Nebuchadnezzar's palace and the famous hanging gardens.

At the temple area itself was the Temple of Marduk, dedicated to the chief Chaldean god, and even more impressive to the north of it the historic Tower of Babel, the place spoken of in the Bible where the confusion of languages took place. It was here that early residents of Babylon started to build a tower that "would reach unto heaven," one also that would give them a name and a reputation.

"And they said," during those early days, "Go to, let us build a city and a tower, whose top may reach unto heaven; and let us make us a name, lest we be scattered abroad upon the face of the whole earth."

The people's effort was thwarted, however, and the tower was never finished until a later date. In the meantime, the spoken language in the area was altered, causing chaos and mass confusion, and thousands of people were dispersed in all directions. "So the Lord scattered them abroad from thence upon the face of all the earth," the Bible says, "and they left off to build the city."[87]

Many centuries passed following the event, and the Tower of Babel went through many different stages, including possible demolitions and rebuildings. In the course of history, it was pillaged and destroyed by Sennacharib of Assyria and Xerxes of Persia, along with others. Consequently, no one really knows what the original tower looked like, although most likely it was some type of Ziggurat. But in one way or another the idea of the Tower was perpetuated

As to what happened to Chaldea and the fortunes of Nebuchadnezzar, it was a different kind of drama, one where something happened very quickly and then disappeared the same way. Unlike the Assyrian Empire, the Chaldean supremacy lasted less than a hundred years before being replaced by Cyrus the

Great and the Persians. Again it was a dramatic episode in history characteristic of the times, a period when the political scene was often in a state of flux and important changes were occurring in the lives of people. Small but significant migrations were taking place in the Middle East at the time, originating in Mesopotomia and Palestine and terminating in far and distant places. Among them was the departure of Lehi from Jerusalem amid the tragic events in the Kingdom of Judah!

Chapter Nineteen

Media

Lehi's family at the time of his exodus consisted of eight people, not counting any sons or daughters that might have been married or away from home. Although the ages of members on that occasion are unknown, it is nevertheless interesting to conjecture what they might have been and in doing so visualize more about the prophet's lifetime, especially regarding the possibility of him being a merchant.

If Lehi's age is theoretically set at 55 years at the time of his departure, for example, this could give him at least thirty-five years in which to be involved in the work field, either as a merchant or in some other occupation. According to this age, those of other family members can then be estimated. As a consequence, the following list of ages might be a reasonable possibility.

Lehi	55
Sariah	45
Laman	21
Lemuel	19
Sam	17
Nephi	15

It is very likely that Lehi had two married daughters at the time, and possibly other married children as well, all of whom had left home. And if this is true, it suggests that he himself might have married at about age 25 and previously had already traveled extensively as a merchant. This would give him plenty of time to begin acquiring considerable wealth, "his gold and his silver and his precious things," and become well acquainted with the Egyptian language.

The idea of him going to such places as Nineveh and Babylon, therefore, and as far away as Egypt and cities along the Mediterranean, is not out of the question. It might definitely be conjectured that long before Lehi was called to the ministry, he was an accomplished student and scholar and had earned a significant reputation as a merchant. He was not just a righteous man, in other words, but one who had been very successful in his profession.

In addition, he undoubtedly benefitted from the traveling he was able to do, which included areas not only in Mesopotamia and the Mediterranean, but places toward the east and as far away as Media. Without overestimating the distances he covered in such areas, once again, the commercial contacts he developed might well have extended as far east as Ecbatana, the Median capital. This was an area familiar to some of the Israelites at least as far back as 721 BC, a century earlier when they were taken into Assyrian captivity.

The Bible tells of people living in central Palestine in 721 who were conquered by Sargon II and deported to various places in the Assyrian Empire, including "the cities of the Medes." Especially with this latter area, people were placed in a mysterious locality which to them was completely unfamiliar and unknown. In identical verses in the Septuagint, the Greek text of the Old Testament, this same area is called "the mountains of the Medes."

"Then the king of Assyria came up throughout all the land, and went up to Samaria, and besieged it three years. In the ninth year of Hoshea the king of Assyria took Samaria, and carried Israel away into Assyria, and placed them in Halah and in Habor by the river of Gozan, and in the cities of the Medes."[88]

Tiglath-pileser III (744–727 BC) and Sargon II (721–705 BC) both deported captives to this part of Media. At the time, the region was literally filled with independent city-states, each with its own leader or ruler. Throughout the extensive mountainous area connecting Assyria with the Median heartland, Tiglath-pileser ravaged a wide swath of territory, deporting an alleged total of 65,000 inhabitants and eventually replacing them with foreign colonists.

The same type of subjugation continued in the reign of Sargon. In 716 BC, for example, five years after the conquest of Samaria, it is recorded that he conducted extensive campaigns in this region and that 28 heads of Median city-states paid tribute to the Assyrian king. Also three years later no less than 45 Median kings gave a similar tribute, most likely as a declaration of allegiance and dependency in regard to Assyria.[89]

The cities of the Medes are also alluded to in the book of Tobias in the Apocrypha which tells about a man named Tobit, an Israelite captive living in Nineveh, who traveled on business to a city called Rages. Later his son Tobias went to the capital city of Ecbatana and met an Israelite girl whom he eventually married. Both of these incidents give brief glances into interactions that allegedly occurred between people in Nineveh and those in nearby Media.

It is interesting to note that Tobit gave a warning to his son on one occasion, reminding him about the prophecies of Jonah and advising him to leave Nineveh and return to Media, which was a safer place. Tobias consequently took his family and traveled to Ecbatana, in which city he was living when he heard that Nineveh had been destroyed.

It was in the land of Media, therefore, where some of the ten tribes spent their time in Assyrian captivity. It was also there during the time of Lehi the prophet that the Median people progressed to a point politically where they could become a state. In the same time period that Nabopolassar and the Chaldeans rebelled against Assyria and proclaimed their independence in Babylonia, a man named Cyaxares did the same thing in Media, unifying the Median people and creating a strong nation and central government.

Prior to that time much had happened among the various tribes and city-states which were scattered throughout the country. The father and grandfather of Cyaxares both were instrumental in preparing a varied group of people for statehood.

Deioces (727–675 BC) was known for his effective leadership and administrative justice and did much to break down the idea of separate tribes and clans in preparation for a united Media. He promoted the concept of a strong monarchy and fortified the capital city of Ecbatana.

His son and successor Phraortes (674–653 BC) continued the same type of program, successfully moving toward a more stable form of government. Whereas Media had earlier been characterized by a multitude of small groups and kingdoms, he now was successful in creating a single and independent governmental system, one that not only met the needs of the people but was capable of resisting the incursions of other people, especially the Assyrians.

It was not just Assyria, however, that was a threat to the Median people. The people known as the Scythians had long been a continuing problem, and for many years they now endangered Media's population and hampered its growth and development. Not until the last part of the seventh century, during the reign of Cyaxares (624–585 BC), was a stable and peaceful situation finally established, one where a Scythian threat was eliminated and the goal of statehood eventually achieved.

It is uncertain how the new king was able to achieve this transformation and new level of government, whether by an alleged trickery against the Scythians or merely by an inherent genius for governing, or both, but what resulted was the appearance of a brand new type of leadership in Media, including a subsequent improvement in the military. Cyaxares made it clear that the new nation would be built not only on the principle of national unity but on that of military power as well. What he had learned from his predecessors was important, but now was the time to accomplish something different, and as the new ruler assumed command, he did not just take control of the government but also in a very short time introduced an impressively new and improved army!

Chapter Twenty

Media

Cyaxares significantly changed the makeup of his armed forces, arranging things so that men and equipment would tactically be more effective. He used innovative methods as well as the proven strategies of the Scythians and Assyrians.

Previously the Median soldiers had gone into battle as tribal groups, all mixed together without any apparent order and each carrying whatever weapon he preferred. Now they were organized into three basic departments of cavalry, archers, and infantry, tactical units based on the types of weapons used.

The Medes were known for their breeding and raising of horses and consequently had an effective and numerous cavalry, all well-trained and adequately equipped. It is said that riders were instructed from childhood how to use a bow and arrow on horseback, being able to shoot accurately from all positions, whether charging an enemy or retreating. Along with foot soldiers, they constituted a formidable weapon and great source of power.

Certainly it was a mark of genius, as well as common sense, when Cyaxares decided to change the complexion of his army. The reorganization and remodeling of the armed forces according to a strategic plan were very successful as he commenced a rigorous program of military operations. The dedication and discipline which he required from his troops caused them to become much like the Assyrians, showing the type of ferocity in battle that was not always typical of soldiers in other countries.

This was apparent in the fighting which took place at the close of the seventh century BC. At the same time that Nabopolassar in Chaldea decided to invade Assyria, Cyaxares and the Medes were thinking of the same thing, each setting as an eventual goal the capital city of Nineveh. The two armies were in northern Mesopotamia during the year 615, moving independently of each other, and in the following year Cyaxares attacked the important city of Ashur on the Tigris River.

Nabopolassar was nearby, but by the time he and his forces arrived at the city, it had already been conquered and plundered by Median soldiers with the type of fury for which they had a reputation. They massacred the inhabitants of the former capital and ruthlessly destroyed its sacred temples, seizing valuable treasures that had been confiscated by the Assyrians from other nations in the Middle East.

The late arrival of the Chaldeans to some extent was very possibly intentional, Nabopolassar not wanting to participate in the wanton destruction of an Assyrian city that had long been a religious center. The desecration of temples and deities revered by people in Babylonia as well as Assyria was not to his liking. The Medes, however, had no such reservation, and they thoroughly sacked the city.

With Ashur burning in the background, Cyaxares and Nabopolassar now agreed to join forces in a combined effort to conquer Nineveh. The sovereigns of the two most powerful countries in the Middle East formed an alliance which virtually assured the demise of Assyria's capital. Nineveh had been the center place for almost a century, but now without question it was about to fall.

As confirmation of the two-nation agreement, a marriage was arranged between the daughter of Cyaxares and Nabopolassar's son. For political purposes Amytis of Media was married to

Nebuchadnezzar of Chaldea. Some say the girl was actually the granddaughter of the king, rather than his daughter, and that she was still a child or even an infant at the time, but whatever the actual circumstances might have been, a royal marriage took place on a historic occasion at the site of a subjugated city.

Two years later in 612 BC the combined attack of Nineveh by Media and Chaldea, and possibly also by the Scythians, took place, and the event that many people in the ancient world had anticipated for so long finally occurred. Between July and August of that year, the doomed capital repulsed three different attacks and yet failed on a fourth as the besiegers broke through the heretofore impregnable walls and ravaged the city. According to tradition the Assyrian king along with members of his family perished in the flames of the burning palace.

Allegedly it was the Median army, rather than the Chaldeans or Scythians, that carried the main attack against Assyria's capital. The subsequent purge was so brutal and complete that the city actually ceased to exist. The invading armies made sure that nothing remained, and in the end Nineveh was reduced to a heap of ashes.

By the close of the year 612, two large Assyrian cities that had been capitals in the past, namely Ashur and Nineveh, were destroyed. The same was possibly true to some degree of Nimrud, and even Dur-Sharrukin or Sargonsburg, as well as many other important towns and cities. Ashur had been the religious metropolis of Assyria, Nineveh the administrative center, and Nimrud the military headquarters. But all three of these historic cities, strung out like beads on a chain along the Tigris River, were now merely skeletons and shadows of the past. Nothing of importance remained except two main cities in northern Mesopotamia where a last attempt at Assyrian survival was made.

Assyria during this later period was led by a man named Ashur-uballit who shortly after Nineveh's downfall proclaimed himself king. He and the remainder of the Assyrian army, and evidently a small force of Egyptians, barricaded themselves in the city of Harran. In the meantime, Cyaxares and the Median armies returned home.

Nabopolassar and the Chaldeans stayed behind, conducting military operations in the area but making no attempt to attack Harran. Then two years later in 610 BC, the king sent a message to Cyaxares in the East for assistance, and in November of the same year the Medes returned, very likely assuming that in Harran there was the opportunity for plunder and a huge amount of booty.

In the siege that followed, Ashur-uballit and the Assyrians offered little resistance, and they soon evacuated their temporary capital and fled westward toward the Euphrates River. The anticipated event then took place in which Cyaxares and his armies entered and pillaged the city of Harran, a city known not only for its reputation as a commercial center and crossroad of transportation, but also a religious mecca dedicated to the moon god, Sin.

From above and below, and the right and the left, according to ancient tradition, the Median invaders appeared like a hurricane, annihilating the Harranites that remained in the city and destroying the sacred Temple of Sin. They showed no mercy as they plundered the famous edifice, also known as the Sanctuary of Ehulhul, and took from it its many treasures. The Chaldeans also participated in the sacrilegious conquest, although their role again is said to have been a subordinate one.

Nabopolassar reportedly prayed to the gods following the unfortunate event, symbolically sleeping on the ground that night instead of in a bed. Like the Temple of the Moon in Ur of the Chaldees, the temple located in Harran was also a sacred place and revered by the Chaldean king. It was difficult for him to deal with the fact that his troops had been involved in its desecration and destruction.

In the Babylonian religion, the moon temple was second in rank only to the more prestigious temple in Ur. Their locations in northern and southern Mesopotamia, both dedicated to the same god, placed them in a unique setting, in a religious sense as well as geographically. Aside from any pagan religion, however, and separate from the relationship which existed between these two temples, there was an even more important situation or circumstance that existed in the same area more than a millennium earlier.

It was in Ur of the Chaldees in southern Mesopotamia where the prophet Abraham left his native country for whatever reason and began an epic journey to Palestine. On his way north he traversed the historic territory of the Tigris and Euphrates Rivers, arriving eventually in Harran where he resided for a time before going on to Canaan. It might only be a coincidence, and then maybe not, that his traveling took him from the site of the southern moon temple to that of the northern. Depending on when these edifices were built, and also related history and circumstances, this type of situation is noteworthy, and if not significant at least interesting, since the scripture exists which tells of Abraham leaving Ur initially because of a dangerous religious environment.[90]

Yet however this might be, and whatever implications it might have, the destruction of the Temple of Sin in Harran by the Medes and Chaldeans in 610 BC remains a significant event in history. Along with the conquest of the capital city of Nineveh and the demise of the Assyrian Empire, it was one of the dramatic events which marked the end of the seventh century and the beginning of the sixth. The reference to Abraham leaving the city of Ur under threatening circumstances is also an important reminder of another historic departure, that of the prophet Lehi whose own migration took him to a place he had never seen before and one which turned out to be a promised land and a place of destiny!

CHAPTER TWENTY-ONE

Media

FOLLOWING THE DESTRUCTION OF HARRAN and the Temple of Sin, Assyria made a valiant attempt in 609 BC to regain the city. Assisted by reinforcements from Egypt, Ashur-uballit besieged his former capital for two months without success and finally was forced to withdraw when he saw the approach of a Chaldean army. No more is known about the Assyrian king except that for the next few years he apparently was fighting in consort with the Egyptians in northern Mesopotamia, their purpose still being to defeat the Medes and Chaldeans, as well as Scythians, and prevent their further incursion into the area. In their support, certain Greek states also appear to have sent military assistance.

Egypt especially showed increased interest during this time period as the Egyptian pharaoh himself appeared on the scene. In 608 BC Necho II and a large army traveled north by way of Palestine to the Euphrates River in an effort to thwart the forces of Nabopolassar and at the same time assist Ashur-uballit. It was definitely to his advantage to keep the Medes and Chaldeans at bay, preserving Assyria as a nation and buffer state and deterring the efforts of the aggressor. Yet in the end it was to no avail since in the year 605 BC, the question of who was dominant in the Middle East was soon resolved.

In Carchemish on the banks of the Euphrates River,

approximately 60 miles west of Harran, a historic battle took place, this time between the Chaldeans and the Egyptians, and undoubtedly Ashur-uballit and the Assyrians as well. The command of the Chaldean armies on this occasion had been transferred from Nabopolassar to his son Nebuchadnezzar, the crown prince of Babylon, and under his aggressive leadership a victory was quickly won. No mention is made of any Median or Scythian participation at the time, only the triumph of Nebuchadnezzar and the Chaldeans.

As things turned out, the Battle of Carchemish was a significant turning point in history and an important landmark in time. Indeed many things were at stake and were resolved in a relatively short period of military operations and combat. What remained of the Assyrian army and Greek mercenaries quickly dispersed, and the Egyptians led by Necho II fled southward toward their own land where they were soon overtaken in the Syrian city of Hamath.

According to one report, the Chaldeans completely liquidated the Egyptian forces, although another source states that after defeating them at Hamath, Nebuchadnezzar continued his pursuit to the borders of Egypt, at which place he received word that his father had died in Babylon. At that point he turned back, evidently arriving at some kind of agreement with Necho as well as stopping in Jerusalem on his return to receive homage and tribute from Jehoiakim, king of Judah.

How Nebuchadnezzar received the urgent message from Babylon concerning his father is unknown, whether by means such as fire and smoke signals or a series of fast couriers, but in approximately one month he covered a distance of about 600 miles to the Chaldean capital, assuming that he traveled from a place like Riplah which was south of Hamath. The battle at Carchemish allegedly began in the summer of 605 BC, and by September of that year the crown prince became the new king of Chaldea in Babylonia.

In the meantime, after all that had happened in Nineveh and northern Mesopotamia, Cyaxares and the Medes began conducting military campaigns of their own. Having conquered Harran and plundered the temple of its copious treasure, the king was content to accept the lucrative spoils of invasion, along with granted territory, and go his own way. Much of his attention was now directed to the north and northwest in what is now Turkey, his conquests including areas known as Urartu, Manna, and Cappadocia.

By 590 BC Cyaxares had occupied land as far west as the Halys River which was near present-day Ankara, Turkey's capital. Here he was confronted by Alyattes, king of Lydia, and for the next five years the two nations engaged in combat for disputed territory. The Lydian ruler was determined to stop Cyaxares from coming into his country, and only the occurrence of what both considered to be a miracle caused them to stop fighting.

History has recorded that on May 28 in the year 585 BC, a solar eclipse took place during one of the Median-Lydian battles and was interpreted by both armies as a bad sign or omen. Consequently the leaders declared a truce in which Cyaxares and Alyattes accepted the Halys River as the official boundary line between the two countries. The daughter of Alyattes was given in marriage to the Median king's son Astyages as a confirmation of their agreement. Once again the ritual of establishing a blood relationship for political purposes was perpetuated.

At the same time, several hundred miles to the southeast in the palace of Nebuchadnezzar, Amytis the Median princess was living out her life as a Chaldean queen. Many years had passed since her own arranged marriage, and in Greek legend and tradition it is said that she longed for her home in the Median mountains, which was vastly different from the environs of Babylonia. The story is that Nebuchadnezzar planted gardens for her on top of his palace, the famous hanging gardens of Babylon, where she could spend time and find solace in her new surroundings. Certainly it was an interesting but sad episode in the life of a young princess.

The hanging gardens consisted of luxurious trees, flowers, and shrubs located on a series of terraces that rose to a height of 300 feet. They were constructed in about 600 BC, according to one account,[91] and required a continuous force of workers pumping water from the Euphrates River for irrigation. Undoubtedly it was one of Nebuchadnezzar's most ambitious and impressive projects, if not his best, and later became known as one of the Seven Wonders of the World. In some ways it was representative of the times, symbolic of the majesty and splendor of kingdoms that existed in the Middle East, particularly that of Nebuchadnezzar during the sixth and seventh centuries BC.

Again this particular age and era of history were more than just a noteworthy period of time. The primary people involved enacted a very unusual drama that was impressive and unique. Indeed it might be said that on occasion it was unprecedented and without parallel. And among the many important figures that might be cited, none are more significant, especially in a religious sense, than the solitary figure of the prophet Lehi who migrated with his family from Jerusalem in 600 BC and began a memorable journey toward a promised land!

Chapter Twenty-two

Egypt

Twelve years before Lehi's departure from Jerusalem, a man named Psamtik I was the pharaoh in Egypt. Also referred to in history as Psammeticus, he was the one who initiated the well-known 26th or Saitic Dynasty, reigning in Egypt for more than a half century. (663–609 BC)

In the beginning of his reign, he was a vassal in the Assyrian Empire, but in approximately 650 BC the new pharaoh took advantage of the current political situation and declared his independence. Ashurbanipal in Assyria was having trouble with Elam and Babylonia at the time, and Psamtik seized the opportunity to rebel. Thus midway through the seventh century commenced a period in Egyptian history regarded as a renaissance or restoration where a nation that had been virtually dormant for centuries suddenly again rose to a position of power and importance and became a force to be reckoned with among the nations.

This was a period of time when Egypt was characterized by a retrospective spirit in which people often were preoccupied with a culture of the distant past. Fascinated by the nation's history dating back to the Old Kingdom and the days of the pyramids, they made a conscious effort to remold some of their social, political, and religious life along ancient lines, imitating a civilization that had existed two millennia earlier. Certainly it was an interesting aspect of Psamtik's administration.

In sharp contrast with the idea of retrospection, however, was Egypt's equally sudden participation in foreign affairs. During this time period the country became active not only in military operations but in commerce and world trade as well.

Having seen the extensive network of commercial activity in the Assyrian Empire and its immense economic value, Psamtik desired the same kind of benefit for his own country. Indeed it was a concept intended not only to improve the present but also prepare for the future. This idea existed simultaneously with the remarkable interest which many people had for things of the past.

Particularly significant during this time was Psamtik's attitude and involvement in things pertaining to the military. Following Ashurbanipal's death, for example, when signs began to appear that the Assyrian Empire was deteriorating, Psamtik's policy toward his former overlord soon changed. Whereas formerly he had been a vassal, he now voluntarily became an ally. In what was probably a surprise to many, he came to the aid of Assyria in the fight against its enemies, evidently wanting to help stem the tide of foreign encroachment.

To the east and northeast the Chaldeans of Babylonia under Nabopolassar had declared their own independence in 625 BC and now planned to invade and conquer parts of upper Mesopotamia. About the same time, the Medes nearby under Cyaxares mobilized their army and prepared to move in the same direction. Also a third group known as the Scythians, originating in the area north of the Black Sea, conducted their own invasions from time to time, and against the power and combined force of these three nations, Egypt decided to cast her lot in defense of Assyria!

It was also during the time of Psamtik and the 26th Dynasty that another circumstance developed, one that was very different from any militarism yet had a significant effect upon many people, including the prophet Lehi and his son Nephi. This was the time in Egyptian history when the type of writing known as demotic came into common usage. The ancient hieroglyphics of the Old Kingdom had long since given way to a cursive script called hieratic, but especially now that administrative and commercial correspondence required something even more practical, the new kind of writing proved to be a remarkable innovation. The demotic, which had first appeared in the eight century, was more condensed and abbreviated and turned out to be a type of shorthand, and was the system that Lehi and his son used for inscribing information upon metal plates.

This particular instance regarding language had a marked effect upon Egyptian culture and was just one of many changes relating to the Saitic Period or 26th Dynasty. Indeed it was part of a dramatic era of history, and some of the changes involved can surely be attributed to the brilliance of one man: Psamtik I who was the dynasty's founder.

Psamtik ruled in Egypt for fifty-four years, and toward the end of that period, in approximately 616 BC, his military forces are known to have been in the north fighting alongside the Assyrians. Again the invaders were Chaldeans, Medes, and possibly Scythians, and in the year 612, after the city of Ashur had earlier been taken by the Medes, the capital city of Nineveh fell before the final onslaught of invading armies. The Assyrians retreated westward to Harran where one of them named Ashur-uballit II proclaimed himself king. In 610 Harran was also conquered and destroyed, and although an attempt was made to regain the city a year later, it was without success.

It is unknown why Egypt was not more active in its support of Assyria at this time, being unable to prevent the conquest and destruction of three of its most important cities. Psamtik might have been hesitant in committing himself too far away from his own capital, and also his age and possible bad health could have been factors. But upon the pharaoh's death in 609 BC, the situation suddenly changed. His son Necho II (609–593

BC) assumed command, and in a short time Egypt increased its military operations.

During the following year, the new pharaoh led an expeditionary force northward toward Assyria in what resulted in a dramatic and unfortunate encounter in the Kingdom of Judah. Josiah was the Israelite king at the time, and what happened is recorded in two different places in the Bible. "In his days, Pharaoh-nechoh king of Egypt went up against the king of Assyria to the river Euphrates," states the record, "and king Josiah went against him; and he (Necho) slew him at Megiddo, when he had seen him."[92]

The brief account in 2 Kings makes it sound as if Necho were going against Assyria, whereas in reality he was traveling to the north in its support. But for whatever reason, Josiah tried to stop him at the place called Megiddo and was killed. The account then says that the king's body was taken to Jerusalem for burial.

But in another biblical account, a more definitive explanation is given as to what might have taken place. For one thing, the pharaoh felt justified in passing through Josiah's territory because, as he put it, the Lord had given him permission to do so.

"Necho king of Egypt came up to fight against Carchemish by Euphrates," the Bible says, "and Josiah went out against him. But he sent ambassadors to him, saying, What have I to do with thee, thou king of Judah? I come not against thee this day, but against the house wherewith I have war: for God commanded me to make haste: forbear thee from meddling with God, who is with me, that he destroy thee not.

"Nevertheless Josiah would not turn his face from him," continues the record, "but disguised himself, that he might fight with him, and hearkened not unto the words of Necho from the mouth of God, and came to fight in the valley of Megiddo. And the archers shot at king Josiah; and the king said to his servants, Have me away; for I am sore wounded.

"His servants therefore took him out of that chariot, and put him in the second chariot that he had; and they brought him to

Jerusalem, and he died, and was buried in one of the sepulchres of his fathers."[93]

In the meantime, the people of Judah, including the prophet Jeremiah, mourned greatly for Josiah, and among these also were undoubtedly Lehi and his family. Josiah was a righteous man and one of Israel's most successful rulers, and the end of his reign marked the beginning of Judah's downfall and eventual destruction. In less than twenty-five years, the Israelite kingdom would fall, not to the Egyptians, but to the Chaldeans of Babylonia. As for Necho, he continued his expedition toward the north to join forces with Ashur-uballit and the Assyrians.

The Valley of Megiddo where Josiah met his defeat was a historic and strategic area in northern Palestine and the Middle East. It was a narrow passageway near the city of Megiddo leading from the plain of Sharon along the Mediterranean coast into the Valley of Jezreel. The passage had been used by caravans and armies for centuries and was a convenient and expedient shortcut to the area of the Jordan River. It is understandable why Josiah would station himself at this point in his attempt to stop Necho.

Regarding the Valley of Jezreel, there is also much of importance, as well as a solemn connection with what happened to Josiah. Another name of the valley, for example, is the Valley of Esdraelon, or Armageddon. It has been a battleground of nations for many hundreds of years and in the future will be the partial site of the famous battle of Armageddon in the book of Revelation. Through the annals of history it is a foreboding place, in striking contrast with its present landscape of peaceful surroundings and fertile crops and fields.

Another question pertaining to Josiah is why he tried to stop Necho from traveling to the north. The more likely answer, of course, is that he was pro-Babylonian in his politics rather than pro-Egyptian, and he wanted to prevent the pharaoh from giving Assyria any help. This was also the view of Jeremiah, and possibly of Lehi. It was not that these men necessarily approved of Nabopolassar or his son Nebuchadnezzar, who were now threatening the Assyrian Empire, but in order to avoid invasion and annihilation, they believed it would be better to submit to the invaders at the outset, which eventually turned out to be true.

Again and again as two of Josiah's sons ruled the Kingdom of Judah during the next twenty-two years, they would unwisely put their trust and confidence in the pharaoh of Egypt. Despite the continued warnings of the prophet Jeremiah, they both ultimately chose to rebel against Nebuchadnezzar, the Chaldean king, and the result was disaster. Neither of the sons followed the example of their father but instead vacillated back and forth in making unwise decisions, completely misjudging the political situation.

"Why gaddest thou about so much to change thy way?" Jeremiah said on one occasion, speaking not only to Judah's rulers but to the nation collectively. "Thou also shalt be ashamed of Egypt as thou wast ashamed of Assyria. Yea, thou shalt go forth from him, and thine hands upon thine head; for the Lord hath rejected thy confidence, and thou shalt not prosper in them."[94] And once again, as it had happened before, it all turned out exactly as the prophet said!

Chapter Twenty-three

Egypt

As Necho arrived in Assyria with reinforcements in 608 BC, there was a renewed effort against the encroachments of Chaldea, Medea, and the Scythians. During the next few years, the Egyptians and Assyrians and their allies made a final attempt to save an empire. For more than a century Assyria had been the ruling nation in the Middle East and beyond, and even though its reputation was now at its lowest ebb, there was still hope that it might survive.

Psamtik I had undoubtedly been reluctant to side with his old enemy toward the end of his reign, yet he had no choice. Realizing what the effect might be if Assyria was replaced by barbaric invaders from the north and east, he chose what he thought was the better alternative, and that was to support the nation that had once ruled over him and keep it as a protective barrier between Egypt and the invading armies. This was also the policy of his son Necho who now significantly increased his country's involvement in what he knew was an alarming situation. In addition, there were others who contributed military forces, such as the nearby Nubians and Libyans and also the Ionian Greeks.

Yet all of the preparations and reinforcements came to naught, for a final battle eventually took place at Carchemish on the banks of the Euphrates River. In an isolated city in northern Syria, a coalition of Egyptians, Assyrians, and mercenaries from other nations established a temporary headquarters and made a heroic last stand, but it was all too late. The Chaldeans from Babylonia, led by their new commander Nebuchadnezzar, completely overwhelmed the defending forces who quickly evacuated the city. Nothing more was ever heard of Ashur-uballit, and Necho's army fled south toward Egypt.

In referring to this historic event, the Bible records both the time and the place. "The word of the Lord which came to Jeremiah the prophet against the Gentiles," the scripture says, "against Egypt, against the army of Pharaoh-necho king of Egypt, which was by the river Euphrates in Carchemish, which Nebuchadnezzar king of Babylon smote in the fourth year of Jehoiakim the son of Josiah king of Judah."[95]

Whether or not the Egyptian king was actually present at the time is unknown, but his forces were overtaken at Hamath where some accounts say they were completely destroyed. Others claim that Nebuchadnezzar pursued at least part of the army to the Egyptian border, stopping only when he suddenly learned of his father's death. At this point the crown prince returned to Babylon where he soon became the new king of Chaldea.

Within a short time, however, he was back in northern Mesopotamia and Syria and from there began attacking areas along the Mediterranean coast from the plain of Sharon to Gaza. His plan was to create an unobstructed passageway to Egypt that would enable him to enter the country and obtain tribute and allegiance from the Egyptian pharaoh. In doing this he subdued one city after another, including the city of Ashkelon, north of Gaza, completely destroying it and deporting many of its people to Babylon.

To the prophet Jeremiah this was all a fulfillment of prophecy. He was delighted to know that Necho had been defeated and had lost face, that the pro-Egyptian party had lost its credibility, and that Egypt itself was now about to be invaded by Nebuchadnezzar.

"Declare ye in Egypt and publish in Migdol," he said, "and publish in Noph (Memphis) and in Tahpanhes (a city in lower Egypt); say ye, Stand fast, and prepare thee, for the sword shall devour round about thee."[96]

It was in the city of Migdol, however, that an important battle eventually took place in approximately 600 BC which undoubtedly surprised Jeremiah, as well as many others, since in this strategic location the Egyptian forces turned back the armies of Chaldea. In a city that was on the northeastern Egyptian border, Necho repulsed Nebuchadnezzar, causing him to return to Babylon. The pharaoh then proceeded northward to Gaza where he took possession of the city.

It was a tremendous victory for Necho and those who supported him, and allegedly he dedicated the armor that he had used in battle to one of Apollo's temples, suggesting that Greek mercenaries, along with certain other foreigners, had been in his army. Definitely it had been common practice since the time of Psamtik for foreigners to serve in the Egyptian armed forces. In any case, what happened at Migdol was a surprising and significant victory for Egypt and caused important repercussions in the Middle East, one of which had to do with the Kingdom of Judah in Palestine.

Jehoiakim was Judah's king at the time and had recently rebelled against the Chaldeans, but when he heard of Nebuchadnezzar's vigorous attacks along the Mediterranean coast, he reconsidered and resumed his payment of tribute. Following the battle at Migdol, however, he again changed his mind. Like his brother Zedekiah who would soon succeed him, he rejected the advice of Jeremiah and again put his trust in Necho, who had organized a strong army in Egypt.

As for Nebuchadnezzar, he discontinued his plans for an Egyptian invasion and instead turned his attention to the Kingdom of Judah, which had rebelled once too often against him. In 597 BC, or in the year 600 by way of Book of Mormon chronology, he entered Jerusalem unchallenged and took possession of the city, installing a new king, Jehoiachin, and reportedly taking 3,000 prisoners. Three months later he placed a different king on the throne, Mattaniah, whose name he changed to Zedekiah, and again took prisoners, this time a reported total of ten thousand. Jehoiakim by this time had apparently died, the exact circumstances of his death being unknown.

A short time before Lehi's departure from Jerusalem, therefore, the Chaldeans deported thousands of prisoners to Babylon, including a deposed king and his family, and also took treasure and booty from the temple and royal palace. Necho, in the meantime, miraculously remained unharmed and secure in his own country. By whatever circumstances and good fortune, he escaped the Chaldean juggernaut and was now free to pursue ventures other than warfare.

At some point in time, possibly soon after his recovery from the Battle of Carchemish, the pharaoh began excavating a canal leading from an eastern branch of the Nile River near present-day Cairo to the Bitter Lakes region further to the east, the length of it being more than fifty miles. From the lakes it was only a short distance south to what is now Suez at the head of the Red Sea. It was a brilliant undertaking for Necho, and had it been completed it would have been a tremendous advantage to Egypt.

Actually the project was one of restoration, since such a canal had been attempted by others in the past. Still it was an ambitious enterprise, and Necho reportedly used 12,000 workers in the process, although the actual number might have been much higher.

The pharaoh eventually discontinued the excavations, the likely reason being that his engineers discouraged him from going any further because of flood danger. The story is that they believed the water level in the Red Sea was higher than that in the Nile Delta. This would consequently cause a problem, they said, once the waterway was completed.

It is unfortunate that Necho listened to the engineers, if this is actually what happened, because his plan for a canal would have been a significant asset for Egypt, not only commercially but in regard to the military as well. During wartime, for example, a waterway connecting the Red Sea with the Mediterranean would provide a valuable strategic advantage.

Also in this same time period, Necho allegedly promoted another idea which potentially was also of great worth to Egypt, namely the circumnavigation of the continent of Africa. Similar to his policy of hiring Greek mercenaries as soldiers, he recruited and dispatched a crew of Phoenician mariners in his employ to sail down the length of the Red Sea. Their three-year journey eventually led them south around the southern end of Africa, up through the Pillars of Hercules or Straits of Gibraltar, and finally back to Egypt.

It was a brilliant accomplishment, if and when it did occur, and the Navy that Necho organized at the time, recruited mainly from Phoenician seamen, might well be one of the most lasting achievements of his reign. With this move, he also established a new African trade route. It was another example of his innovation and vitality as a leader, not just in the military but also in the area of trade and commerce. And although his image has sometimes been tarnished by those who say he had a bad reputation and was a warlike pharaoh, the account given in the Bible once again, at the time he killed Josiah, gives evidence that would suggest otherwise.

Necho tried to avoid hurting the king on that occasion, saying he meant him no harm and that his quarrel was with someone else. He even attempted to prevent a showdown by claiming that God himself had given his approval for the pharaoh to pass through Judah's territory. There was no indication of any hostility or brutality, in other words, but rather the character of someone more apt to show reasonability and compassion. And yet the judgment of history has still been unkind to him, and when he died in 593 BC, after having reigned in Egypt for more than fifteen years, he did not receive the kind of praise and acclamation that had been given to his father!

Chapter Twenty-four

Greece

When Necho turned back the invasion of Nebuchadnezzar at Migdol, as the Chaldeans attempted to enter Egypt, it was undoubtedly surprising to many that the pharaoh had assembled a strong army so quickly. The battle took place at the end of the seventh century BC or at the very beginning of the 6th, and only five years earlier at Carchemish in the year 605, the Egyptian forces had supposedly been decimated.

The event at Migdol was a good example of Necho's resilience and determination, as well as his ability as a military commander. It was also evidence that he had access to a considerable amount of manpower from which to recruit armed forces, including the valuable help he obtained from other nations.

Greek mercenaries especially, who apparently were at Carchemish as well as Migdol, made up a significant part of the Egyptian army. Both Necho and Psamtik I were indebted to them during military operations. Again it is said that following the battle at Migdol, for example, Necho dedicated his personal battle armor to the god Apollo at one of the Greek temples.

It was at this time in history that Greek traders and settlers were also active, expanding throughout the Mediterranean and Black sea regions in a vast movement of colonization. Motivated by economic pressures and a need for new land, they migrated into many different areas. Sometimes colonizers followed those who had been hired to serve in the military, but in one way or another, the Greek presence soon became widespread. Certainly it was the beginning wave of a particular culture and influence that eventually would affect the entire ancient world.

The genesis of this movement was centered especially in the important city-states on the Greek mainland, the largest and most notable being Sparta, Athens, Argos, and Thebes. Besides being called states, these areas were also regarded as nations, each being small in territory but having its own specific characteristics and form of government. Undoubtedly it was Sparta and Athens who were at the forefront, however, since in these two areas Greece in some ways found its most meaningful expression.

The two nations occupied very different positions, both geographically and politically. Sparta was located in what was known as the Peloponnesus, a huge island connected with the mainland by only a small isthmus of land. Athens nearby was at the head of a long peninsula and situated near the seacoast. Both groups had their own form of government, differing markedly from one another, and their presence in the overall Greek culture and civilization presents an extremely unusual picture during the 600 BC period. In Sparta especially there developed a very unique type of society.

As late as midway through the eighth century, the Spartans in the Peloponnesus were no different from any other Greek state, although for whatever reason they chose to participate very little in outside colonization. Instead they invaded the territory of Messenia immediately to the west and after a lengthy war from approximately 730–710 BC were victorious in appropriating a large volume of new land. Sparta's king on this occasion was named Theopompos (c. 720–675), and as a result of the victory, an increased number of helots or serfs came under his jurisdiction.

The type of government at the time was extraordinary in that there were two kings instead of one, each ruling concurrently with the other. One of these was Polodoros (c. 700–665), and it was evidently toward the latter part of his reign that a certain event occurred in Sparta which dramatically changed the course of its history. The serfs in Messenia, aided by Argos, Arcadia, and the Pisatans, all residents in the Peloponnesus, staged a massive revolt, and for the next twenty years Sparta again was at war. Earlier in 669 BC it had been defeated decisively in battle by Argos at a place called Hysiai, and it was this particular event which might have prompted the Messenians to revolt.

Spartan history during this early time period, relating to specific dates and individuals, is extremely brief, but it was about this time that a man named Tyrtaeus became prominent in the country's affairs. He was not only a well-known poet and statesman but also an able military commander, and behind his leadership Sparta finally subdued the Messenians once again and paved the way for a radical and revolutionary change in government and way of life, a movement that very possibly commenced in about 600 BC.

Again the historical account is brief, and it is often indefinite as to when a certain event occurred, but sometime following the second Messenian War, the Spartan nation adopted a new system of government and embarked upon a new era socially, politically, and economically. It was an elaborate program that was very regimented and one that especially involved the military. In a giant movement of reformation, an individual named Lycurgus made his appearance in history with the purpose of stabilizing the country and preventing any further rebellion or revolution by the Messenians. Whether he was a symbolic figure or an actual person is not known, but in any case, he indelibly inscribed his name on Spartan history as a great hero, lawgiver, and administrator and initiated a radically new governmental system.

The Spartan kings at the turn of the century, continuing the reigns of two royal houses of Agiad and Eurypontid, were Eurykratidas (c. 615–590) and Leotychidas I (c. 625–600).

Hippokratidas (c. 600–575) also ruled during this time period. Even though very little is known about these kings, they nevertheless were the ones who evidently were at the head of Sparta's government when the Lycurgus reforms began to take place.

The reforms once again were mainly directed toward national security. Most of those living in Sparta were helots or serfs, including people acquired through conquest, and the primary aim of the new government, along with a new constitution, was to build a strong military state patterned after a type of communism that could best control the serfs. The Spartan citizenry, the male members of which made up only about one-tenth of the total population, almost totally turned their backs on an easy way of life, substituting in its place a life of abstinence and self discipline pertaining to things of comfort and luxury.

In accomplishing this they transformed what had been a normal society enjoying a conventional lifestyle into what now resembled a military camp. Indeed the government's plan was to create a military machine that would produce what Sparta considered to be the ideal citizen, someone who possessed the qualities and characteristics that could help ensure the nation's security, both within the country and without. And in this they proved successful. It is no wonder that centuries later in a modern society, someone might regard a person with a Spartan character as one who is frugal and self-disciplined, having a stoic attitude and abstaining from anything associated with luxury and pleasure.

In order to implant the new system into Sparta's culture, therefore, every important aspect of daily life was placed under state direction and control, and nowhere was this more apparent than in public education. At age seven a young boy was taken from his mother or nurse and placed in a strict training program with other youths. Here they lived in barracks and were initiated into a life of military drill and exercise, designed to develop obedience, courage, toughness, and physical strength. Once a year, as part of the curriculum, each boy also submitted to a supreme test of endurance where he was given a severe flogging. Emphasis was always placed upon the type of instruction that would engender the attributes of a good soldier.

Upon reaching age twenty, a boy was regarded as a man and consequently became eligible for active military service. He could marry now, although married life was much different from what was normal, and the time that he spent with his wife might have been only by stealth. Certainly during his late childhood and growing-up years, he had never experienced a regular home, and even as a man his life was mainly one of military drill, eating, and sleeping in the barracks. It was a lifestyle probably not envied or desired by other Greeks, even though the Spartan as an individual was often admired.

The women of Sparta were also held in esteem. Girls went through a training similar in some ways to that of the boys, and they were known throughout Greece for their physical strength and beauty, as well as courage and athletic prowess. Undoubtedly they were in noticeable contrast with other women such as those in nearby Athens or Corinth.

In regard to physical ability, it is interesting to note how the Spartans fared in the Olympic Games, held every four years at Ellis in the northwestern Peloponnesus. Allegedly they produced about one-half of the victories prior to 600 BC, predominantly in racing events and the pentathlon. Yet subsequent to that date, they showed a marked decline in Olympic championships, which at first might seem surprising since this particular time period was also the approximate date that Sparta's unusual reform began, a program that placed so much importance on physical strength and ability.

And yet this was also the time when professional athletes began to appear, and because the Spartans stressed guts, toughness, and endurance in opposition to the technology and fine art of sports, they eventually put themselves at a disadvantage. It became more and more difficult to compete against professional athletes who approached athletic contests more scientifically. In a way it was equivalent to a fight between a man who was armed and one that was unarmed, or in other words a competition between experienced athletes and non-professionals. In refutation of this advantage, however, the Spartan would likely say that an over-specialized athlete might win in the Olympics but probably would not make a good soldier.

But however it might have been, Sparta's new program was highly successful throughout the country and gave every indication that it was there to stay. The serfs were under control and providing revenue for financing the government and supporting the citizenry, and an educational system was in process where youth from ages seven to twenty were indoctrinated and trained to be soldiers. Everything proceeded in a way that was intended, and by the time a man reached thirty years of age he was in the prime of his life, ready to receive full Spartan citizenship and participate more actively in the affairs of government. He was still a member of the armed forces, and would continue to be until age sixty, but in the meantime his life was probably more normal, even though most of the time he was preoccupied with things of the military.

Certainly it is significant that all of this was taking place on the mainland of Greece during the time of 600 BC and that one of the city-states should conceive of a concept and idea like the one put forth under the name of Lycurgus. Without question it was a daring experiment, observed with interest throughout the Peloponnesus and surrounding nations, and although as a social system it did not compare well with others as far as contributions to civilization was concerned, it did for two centuries produce what has been regarded as the strongest land power among the Greeks, as well as the most stable government. The courage and competence expressed in the military especially would be important during future attacks by the forces of Persia.

Yet in addition to all that might be said about Sparta as a nation, it was the effect which the country's reformation had upon the individual citizen, both male and female, that was particularly significant. Despite the fact that his or her importance was subordinate to the welfare of the state, a type of character developed toward the end of the seventh century BC that might well be termed distinctively Spartan.

Such individuals were not only characterized by physical strength and endurance but ironically also by a modest demeanor, a certain politeness and courtesy existing along with the toughness. One example, if it is true, is something that happened one day at the Olympic Games. As the story goes, an old man was attempting to find a place to sit, and the crowd for some reason jeered at him. It was only when he came to where the Spartans were sitting that men and boys alike stood up to offer him a seat. The crowd in the stadium applauded when they saw it, causing the man to remark that all Greeks knew what was right, but only the Spartans actually did it.

Again an individual from Sparta, whether it was a man or a woman from the regular citizenry or ruling class, was often noticeably different from other people. Undoubtedly it was the specific reflection of how a person had been raised, stemming from principles such as personal obedience, allegiance to a cause, self-denial, and a deliberate contempt of pleasure. But whatever it was, it was something that gave an important meaning to life and caused one to be proud that he was a Spartan.

And although it was said sometimes that the average person in this part of Greece was a nonintellectual who lacked creativity and innovation, especially in areas such as art and literature, a Spartan might be apt to say that his country did not create things in wood and stone, but rather in men and women. Indeed the purpose of Lycurgus from the beginning had been not just to suppress rebellion among the serfs but in the very process to create the ideal Greek citizen. In an attempt to do this, the Spartans might not always have been successful yet in a heroic effort were nevertheless admired and respected for their dedication to a cause and a willingness to sacrifice so much to achieve it!

Chapter Twenty-five

Greece

Whether or not the prophet Lehi ever traveled as far west as Sparta is unknown, but it is doubtful because the Spartans generally discouraged interaction with other countries, and especially if Lehi was a merchant, he might have found it difficult getting across the Spartan border. Inasmuch as the Lycurgus reforms tried to keep foreign ideas and influence out of the country, any outside visitor probably would not have been welcome.

In the city-state of Athens, however, there was a much different situation, and the likelihood is that Lehi very possibly visited this part of Greece, which would have given him not only an opportunity for travel but also important commercial contacts, if indeed he was a merchant. Athens was located on the Attic Peninsula across the gulf from Sparta, and although the distance separating the two areas was only about a hundred miles, the difference between the cultures was tremendous.

From the beginning it seemed as though Athens was marked for some kind of special destiny. Its particular civilization and culture, combined with a gradual progression toward democracy, established it in many ways as a model state that would often be used as a guide and pattern by others in the future.

And yet Athens went through the same kind of early development as other city-states, including a colonization period extending from the eighth to the sixth centuries BC, as well as an important transition from monarchies to aristocracies. Moreover the latter part of this time was also one when so-called tyrants began to appear in Greece. These were not despotic rulers who subjected people to a traditional type of tyranny but instead men who disapproved of how nobles of the aristocracy were handling the government and consequently intervened and substituted a more practical political system. One who attempted to do this was an Athenian noble named Cylon in approximately 632 BC.

Cylon was a member of one of the most powerful families in Athens and had gained recognition and popularity by winning a championship event in the Olympic Games. He was also the son-in-law of Theagenes, the ruling tyrant in Megara which was the city-state immediately west of Athens.

With the support of mercenary soldiers sent by Theagenes along with a group of followers from the nobility, Cylon challenged the Athenian government and tried to install himself as a new ruler. To accomplish this he seized control of the Acropolis, the large outcropping of rock overlooking the city, and took refuge in the Temple of Athena. From earliest times the Greeks had used this hilltop as a fortress and religious center, as well as a bartering place, and it was here that the revolutionaries confronted government troops that stormed up from below.

Two hundred years would pass before the construction of the temples known as the Parthenon and Erechtheum, one on the south side of the Acropolis and the other on the north. Both of these buildings contained statues of the goddess Athena, the Parthenon especially being well known and publicized in modern times. The statue in this particular temple was approximately forty feet in height and made of ivory and gold, making it one of the most revered deities among the Greeks.

It was Athena's temple in Cylon's time, however, where he and his people now assembled for protection. In the invasion that followed, some say that Cylon himself escaped, but in any case, the people that remained finally surrendered and agreed to a settlement. The government forces said they would spare the rebels' lives if they would come down and stand trial, which terms the rebels accepted, and yet what took place as they descended from the Acropolis resulted in a strange and unfortunate drama.

Before leaving the temple, the people tied a thread to Athena's statue and held to it as they walked into the valley below. The idea was they would be protected as long as they kept the thread intact, but at a certain place along the way it snapped, and at that point most of the people were attacked and slain. It was an unfortunate event, thereafter referred to as the Cylonian pollution, and because of it the man who ordered the massacre, along with his family, was cursed by the gods, or so the people believed, and as a consequence he and his family were exiled from Athens.

What happened at the Acropolis that day was not only repulsive to the Athenian people, but in addition it caused many of them to lose respect for the ruling nobles of the aristocracy. In no way could they justify the action taken against those who had sought refuge at an altar or sacred place. It was just one more reason for discontent and dissatisfaction with the government.

The social and economic problems in Athens, similar to what existed in other places in Greece, were overwhelming to the majority of people. More and more the lower classes were exploited by those who were above them, losing land and property and in many cases personal freedom. It was not uncommon for a man to borrow money at a high interest rate or to mortgage his farm in order to pay off a debt, and even offer himself as collateral for a loan, which often resulted in slavery.

Moreover there was dissatisfaction as well as suspicion concerning the laws by which people were supposed to be governed. No one really knew what the laws were since they were not written for everyone to see, and the citizens often were at the mercy of the nobles in regard to individual rights and protection.

Because of this, and in response to public pressure, the

government finally gave special permission and authority to a man named Draco and instructed him to implement necessary improvements in the legal system and to codify the laws, making them known for the first time in written form to the people. This historic event took place in the year 621 BC.

Draco's laws were unusual in that they were so strict and severe. The intent was to assure the protection of life and property and to impress upon people's minds the importance of obeying the law, even when it pertained to situations that might be considered trivial. Capital punishment, for example, was given not only for sacrilege and murder, but also for such offenses as petty theft and idleness. For people living in poverty, stealing fruit and vegetables was a serious offense, but still for one to be condemned to death for taking a cabbage or an apple seemed unreasonably extreme.

Someone is said to have exclaimed at one time that Draco's laws were not written in ink, but in blood. It is understandable how a new word eventually came into the vocabulary because of his code, namely Draconic or Draconian, meaning "harsh" or "severe."

And yet in spite of the strictness, the laws proposed by Draco represented a significant advance in criminal justice and the improvement of the legal system. No longer were people at the disadvantage of having only oral laws. Now the laws were clearly defined and written. Also in adopting a specific code, the city-state government assumed greater responsibility for the public welfare. Appropriate courts were established to deal with civil and criminal cases in a more systematic manner. Although there were still flaws in the system, it proved to be an innovative piece of legislation and a definite improvement as far as the commoners and lower classes were concerned.

But the plight of the people still continued, and it was obvious that something different needed to be done to change a deteriorating economic condition. It was also evident that Athens desperately needed someone who could step forward at this particular time and provide a unique kind of leadership, one who could arbitrate between the nobles on the one hand and the people of Athens and Attica on the other. And as it turned out, such a person finally did appear, a man named Solon (c. 639–559 BC) who had outstanding ability and many talents and became well known as a general, fighting on the island of Salamis off the coast of Greece.

Reference to Solon is especially important because he was an exact contemporary of Lehi, and having traveled widely as a trader or merchant he very possibly knew about the prophet during an earlier time period. The idea that Lehi met Solon in Athens or in some other part of Greece on business, even elsewhere such as Egypt or the Middle East, is only speculation, but nevertheless a possibility.

In regard to Solon's affiliation with the Athenian military, however, and consequently his involvement in politics, the historical account concerning him definitely begins at Salamis, an island immediately west of Attica and situated between Athens and the city-state of Megara. Its location offshore and in close proximity to the Corinthian Gulf gave it strategic importance in trade and commerce and was often a matter of dispute between Athens and its neighbor. At the time that Solon became a principal figure in Athens, the island was in Megara's possession, and because the Athenians had spent so much time recently to secure it without success, a law was passed saying that anyone trying further to do so would be subject to the death penalty.

But Solon was not one to give up easily, and in spite of the risk and danger involved, he allegedly concocted an ingenious plan that would authorize him to go to war with Megara once again and obtain the island of Salamis. His strategy in accomplishing this was to pretend he had temporarily lost his mind, after which he went into the marketplace one day and began to recite poetry, verse after verse, in which he espoused the idea of continuing the war for the sake and honor of Athens and eventually conquering Salamis.

Among other things, Solon was a poet. He had composed the verses ahead of time and then recited them in a way that appeared to be unpremeditated and extemporaneous. The people interpreted what he said as an expression of divine will, and the law prohibiting war with Megara was repealed. Solon was then appointed as general and given command of a new expedition to Salamis.

Although such an event has been called into question historically, whatever actually happened evidently worked, for history records that the Athenians finally acquired the island, at least for a time, and Solon earned prestige and notability as a leader. It was a significant occurrence that took place in approximately 610 BC and enhanced his reputation not only as a military commander but later also as a politician, statesman, philosopher, and poet.

In the years that followed, Solon established himself as an important figure in the government. Being a moderately rich noble among the upper class, and one of the most respected men in the country, he was elected to the high office of archon in 594 BC and given supreme power to improve economic conditions throughout Attica, including giving immediate assistance to the peasants. From the very beginning he appeared to have had no greater purpose than to alleviate the condition of that part of the population who had been mistreated and held in subjection for more than a century.

Soon after entering office, he legislated a law freeing all those who were in slavery because of debt, both at home and abroad. In addition, he emphasized that no one in the future would be permitted to offer himself as security for a loan or implicate any member of his family. In commemoration of his extraordinary emancipation of the slaves, therefore, the people showed appreciation to Solon by holding an annual feast and celebration in Athens in his honor.

To ensure the success of his legislation, Solon abolished all securities on both land and person and cancelled all personal debts. Commercial debt still needed to be paid, but the fact that Athenian citizens, at whatever social level, were now free and able to start anew in many ways was a tremendous and remarkable event.

Significant also were the changes that Solon made in Draco's laws. Although he left penalties pertaining to homicide as they were, he reduced others that were obviously too severe, particularly those in regard to petty crimes. He also recalled from exile people who had been unjustly banished from the country. For these and other such achievements, Solon became known throughout Greece and surrounding areas, not just as an able administrator and legislator but also a great humanitarian, a noble liberator and emancipator of the slaves. In achieving this recognition, not only did he benefit people in Athens and throughout Attica, particularly those among the lower classes and peasantry, but even more importantly helped lay the groundwork for a future democracy and democratic government!

Chapter Twenty-six

Greece

Before leaving office as an archon, Solon made several changes in the Athenian constitution that greatly favored the lower classes. Again these people appeared to be his main concern while he served in the government and military and throughout the general time period of 600 BC. Surely it had been the trademark of his administration to champion the rights of the commoners and peasants. He was especially interested in preventing people from falling into slavery again.

For the first time by way of legislation, Solon made it possible for citizens in the lower classes to obtain membership in what was known as the Assembly, which among other things gave them a voice in passing laws and electing public officers and magistrates. This was a highly significant change of policy and an important innovation in government. But it was the creation of the Heliaea, or supreme court, that was possibly Solon's most far-reaching achievement. Qualified people from all social classes who were over thirty years of age, including the peasantry, became eligible for admission into this august body, one that was foremost in laying the foundations of a future democracy.

An important function of the Heliaea was to receive appeals concerning decisions made by the archons, by which the people themselves became a court of last resort. It also tried magistrates for misconduct in office, if and when it occurred. Never before had these kinds of things taken place, and it was to Solon's credit that they were now incorporated into the government. Consequently his name came to be synonymous with wisdom and political acumen so that in modern times lawmakers have often been referred to as "solons."

Finally, at a point when he could have declared himself as tyrant and ruled for many years in Athens, Solon suddenly relinquished his position as archon and decided to spend the next several years traveling, visiting places in the Middle East and eventually Egypt. It was a time of respite for him and an opportunity to visit new places and meet new people. One of the first stops on his long itinerary was Miletus in what is now western Turkey. Here he allegedly met Thales (c. 640–546 BC), a famous philosopher, mathematician, astronomer, and statesman, and one who was another important contemporary of the prophet Lehi.

Speculation that Lehi might have been about age 55 at the time of his departure from Jerusalem would make him approximately ten years older than both Solon and Thales. It would in turn make him a meaningful contemporary and provide ample time to have interacted with either or both of them. Because they were notable personalities in Greece's history and culture, the prophet's attention during an earlier time period would naturally have been drawn to them.

In regard to Thales himself, one of the important incidents in his life, and consequently a well-known claim to fame, was something that happened shortly after the time that Lehi left Jerusalem, namely his prediction of a solar eclipse in 595 BC, or 598 according to Book of Mormon time. This was the spectacular event which occurred while Cyaxares of Media was engaged in battle with Alyattes of Lydia on May 28 of that year, causing them to be wary of an unusual sign in the sky and to declare a truce at the end of five years of fighting in the area of the Halys River in present-day Turkey.

It was also in Turkey, in the west coast city of Miletus, that an interesting encounter is said to have taken place between Thales and Solon sometime after the latter departed from Athens. Solon asked him one day, as the story goes, why it was he had never married and raised a family. At the time, Thales gave no answer but later arranged for someone to meet his friend and pretend he was a stranger who had recently returned from a visit to Athens.

Being interested if there was any news from home, Solon enquired what had been happening there, and during the conversation the stranger mentioned that there had been a certain funeral which the entire city attended. Solon asked who had died, but the man said he only knew that it was the son of someone who had left Athens for a time and was traveling.

This alarmed Solon, of course, and he remarked how miserable it must be for one who had just lost a son. Again he quizzed the stranger, asking if he knew the name of the boy's father. But the man said he knew nothing more than what people had told him, which was that he was an honorable man in the city and well-known for his wisdom and justice. With each answer to a question, therefore, Solon became more anxious and distraught, and finally he asked the stranger if by any chance the funeral was for the son of a man named Solon, to which the man replied that that was the name.

Thales was nearby when Solon heard the news, and as the latter responded in an understandable way, showing great anguish and grief, his friend walked over to him and took his hand. "These things, Solon," he told him with a smile, "keep me from marriage and rearing children, which are too great for even your constancy to support; however, be not concerned at the report," he said, "for it is a fiction."[97]

Such was a memorable occurrence, possibly true and maybe not, but in any case it is a story that brings together two outstanding figures in an interesting way, two men both from Greece who had an extraordinary impact upon history. One became well-known for political achievement and statesmanship, the other for scientific accomplishment and philosophy, and together with another figure far away in Palestine whose name was Lehi, a man destined to be a great prophet and religious reformer, the three men form an interesting trio. And whether or not their paths actually crossed during their lifetimes, each in his own way contributed much to the course of society, and it will always be significant that the three were so closely contemporary with one another!

Chapter Twenty-seven

Rome

Several hundred miles west and northwest of Athens are the famous seven hills of Rome. It was here toward the end of the seventh century BC, possibly very close to the year 600, that an event took place which eventually had a highly important impact on the people of the ancient world.

Long before the time of the Roman Empire, a group of villages on the banks of the Tiber River in central Italy were united for the first time in what might be called the city of Rome. The hills and intervening ravines on which they were located were about fifteen miles east of the Tyrrhenean Sea, a large branch of the Mediterranean. No one could have known at that time that this area would someday be the center and capital of the civilized world, but undoubtedly this was the place where it started, and the beginning date again was allegedly about 600 BC.

The seven hills were only sparsely populated at first, but eventually they became the hub of social and political activity. Three of them were closest to the river, these being known later as the Capitoline, Palatine, and Aventine. The others, located a short distance away, were mainly spurs or promontories and were called the Quirinal, Veminal, Esquiline, and Caelian.

In this compact area, therefore, the place known as Rome or Roma had a beginning. Prior to its being an established, politically recognized city, the region had been ruled by four legendary kings whose identity in history often remains obscure, they in turn being followed by three others that are more well-known and historical. These two categories of rulers might be regarded as Roman monarchy during the eighth to sixth centuries BC, before as well as after the establishment of an actual city.[98]

Romulus	c. 753–716
Numa Pompilius	c. 716–672
Tullus Hostilius	c. 672–640
Ancus Martius	c. 640–616
Tarquin the Elder	c. 616–578
Servius Tullius	c. 578–534
Tarquin the Proud	c. 534–510

Such a king list suggests that when Lehi the prophet left Jerusalem in 600 BC, the first real king of Rome was a man named Tarquin the Elder, also referred to in history as Lucius Tarquinius Priscus. The commencement of his reign has been placed as late as 607 BC, although the more common date is 616, and it is said that he ruled for 38 years. Certainly it is characteristic of this particular time period for scholars and historians to differ in many ways, but beginning with this particular king, the historical record is much more accurate and secure.

Tarquinius Priscus ruled at a time when people known as the Etruscans were a dominant force in the ancient Italian peninsula. Having theoretically immigrated from Asia Minor in the East, they were a very civilized group compared to the native population, and whether or not Tarquinius was one of them, being Etruscan by birth, or an outsider who rose to a position of authority, he was nevertheless an able administrator, as well as an aggressive military commander. Recorded events and corresponding dates are scarce during this era of Roman history, but there are still certain situations and occurrences that give important information and provide an interesting background to the time of Lehi and his historic departure from Jerusalem.

The identity and sequence of events are not always clear, but early in the reign of Tarquinius he appears to have been at war with hostile neighbors, mainly with groups known as the Latins and also people who were called Sabines. There were several such conflicts in which the new king was victorious, and gradually the idea was established that a different spirit or influence was operating in the peninsula, one where Etruscan leadership was now in command. An implication was that the Etruscans had an important mission to perform during the sixth and seventh centuries BC, which was to instruct and further civilize the Latins or Romans.

In addition to military conquests, Tarquinius also commenced a mammoth building project, designed to convert Rome from a group of small villages with huts to a large city with imposing buildings and temples. To accomplish this he reclaimed the extensive swampland around the seven hills, draining water into the Tiber River, and thus creating additional public and private real estate. He also started building a wall around the proposed dimensions of the city.

All of this was an expression not only of an ambitious ruler's foresight and leadership but in addition the advanced culture he represented. Whereas the Romans had earlier been a relatively backward group compared to places like Athens, Nineveh, and Babylon, and certainly cities like Memphis and Jerusalem, they now became a much more sophisticated and progressive people. More and more they deemed it important to acknowledge that they were not just Latins or Etruscans but Romans. They possessed a new identity, in other words, and a new spirit.

But it was the building program where Tarquinius visibly expressed his ideal for a noble city. Between the Capitoline and Palatine hills he leveled the ground for a new Forum, an area that became the central and principal place in Rome beyond any public place that previously had been known. In this specific location there was a focal point for centuries to come, an area accommodating social, political, religious, and economic activity. Indeed in no other place in the Roman government, whether in the present monarchy or in a future republic and empire, was there a location more important and significant than the Forum.

Equal in importance in some ways was the area which developed on the crest of the Capitoline. Here Tarquinius commenced the construction of a magnificent temple that he had pledged to build while fighting a war with the Sabines. It honored the deities known as Jupiter, Juno, and Minerva, the equivalents in Greek mythology of Zeus, Hera, and Athena. Tradition states that it was the first major monument to be built in the city and was revered by the Romans as their most sacred sanctuary.

The temple on top of the Capitoline, therefore, was where the ancient Romans worshipped Jupiter as the most powerful of their gods. Within a walled enclosure and on a sacred altar, priests offered religious sacrifices and celebrated military victories, ceremonies that made this particular hill and the Palatine the two most famous hills in Rome.

Still there was one more place that was especially important in the area, a location situated between the Palatine and Aventine hills. At this point Tarquinius marked out what was to become the Circus Maximus, the greatest of all Roman stadiums and a facility which for the next thousand years would be the most popular entertainment center in the city. The structure was oblong in shape and eventually seated more than 200,000 spectators. In this huge arena, which was enlarged and made more magnificent in subsequent years, the Romans witnessed chariot races and other athletic events that helped make their city famous. Along with military victories and the building enterprises occurring at the end of the seventh century BC and the beginning of the sixth, the creation of the Circus Maximus, in addition to the new Forum and the temple on the Capitoline, constituted what now might be called the actual founding of the city of Rome.

Certainly the reign of Lucius Tarquinius Priscus, alias Tarquin the Elder, stands out in history as a very meaningful and important time. Not only was it significant for those living on the Italian Peninsula but also in other parts of the Mediterranean world as well. In particular it had a special meaning in regard to Lehi, the man who at this time was about to depart from Jerusalem or was already on his way to a location somewhere on the shoreline of the American continent. During the same years that the foundations were laid for what later became known as Rome and the Roman Empire, a system of government in which one nation laid claim to the entire civilized world, a Judean prophet and his company prepared to open up a new world of their own, one that in some ways would be even more unique and outstanding than that created by the Romans!

Chapter Twenty-eight

Conclusion

There were eight people during the 600 BC period who related significantly to the prophet Lehi, eight individuals from different countries who in one way or another interacted meaningfully with the prophet's lifetime. All were leaders or heads of state and exact contemporaries, each one having a plan or objective, or at least a responsibility, in guiding his particular nation to some goal or destiny, whatever it might have been. Eight people came forward at a very specific time in history to serve as Lehi's backdrop, and although they differed from one another in many ways, they all had at least one thing in common, and that was that each person, depending on his nationality, not only had an avowed goal or purpose, but also a dream.

While accomplishing this, each one contributed in his own way to a complex matrix of events and circumstances that was a significant part of Lehi's historic departure. In eight different regions in the Middle East and along the Mediterranean, these people were the contemporaries of an Israelite prophet who also had a dream and who shared the same hope and resolve that somehow it would be a polestar leading to a better world and future.

Judah

Zedekiah was in his first year as king of Judah when Lehi left Jerusalem, and undoubtedly his own particular dream had to do with the urgent political situation and precarious position of his country. He was just a young man at the time, only twenty-one years of age, and the Kingdom of Judah was presently a conquered nation, being subject to the king of Chaldea in Babylon.

A short time earlier the armies of Nebuchadnezzar had entered Jerusalem and deposed the previous king, taking him and many Israelite prisoners into captivity and installing a new ruler. And although Zedekiah gave his oath and made a covenant that he would be subservient, he always remained in doubt as to what he should do.

It was against his feeling and disposition to submit to the barbarian invaders from the north, and his main hope was that somehow he could avoid it by soliciting the protection of Egypt. In doing so he would still be a subordinate, but as an Egyptian vassal there would be a more meaningful relationship. At least this was his dream.

Israel

The situation was much different among those in the Kingdom of Israel, which had been conquered more than a hundred years earlier by the Assyrians. Many of these people were taken to places of captivity, but at least some at a later time traveled further into the north countries, searching for a place where they could escape from surrounding nations and be by themselves.

One of the captives was undoubtedly the group's leader, and whoever he was, and whatever his name might have been, he was the one who likely had the dream. According to scripture, God himself was leading the group, but always there is the implication that someone like unto Moses was at the forefront guiding Israelites of a different time period to some kind of promised land.

The individual who finally made the announcement that a signal had been given and it was time for them to leave, undoubtedly had some kind of vision or premonition of where they were going. In a time of need, and when something of great importance is involved, there is usually someone who is called or steps forward with a plan and accepts the responsibility to lead. Among those known as the ten lost tribes, this was such a man.

Assyria

In the case of Assyria, it was an unknown figure named Ashur-uballit who appeared almost out of nowhere in an attempt to save his country and assumed command of an army thought to be defeated and non-existent. At a time when it seemed that the Assyrian Empire had fallen, the last king having perished in a palace fire, one who might have been one of the king's nobles refused to give up. With the dream and confidence that something could still be done, he declared himself the new ruler and led his forces westward from the burning capital of Nineveh to a new location where for several years he continued to fight.

It would have been easy for him on that occasion to be overwhelmed by the combined forces of Chaldea and Media, and possibly the Scythians. Certainly their intent was to destroy a nation that had long ruled with force and cruelty throughout the Middle East. But Ashur-uballit persevered and for a time still dreamed of saving an empire.

His effort was to no avail, however, and even with the help of Egypt and an army of mercenaries, he eventually disappeared without admitting defeat. History never recorded that he was captured or killed, but his legend lived on, even though his dream had come to an end.

Chaldea

Nebuchadnezzar was still a crown prince when he acquired full command of the armies of Chaldea, but upon his father's death, he was crowned the new ruler and became what the Bible refers to as king of Babylon, a "king of kings" and the visionary "head of gold." Indeed very few people in biblical scripture have received more attention than this particular man.

From the beginning, he harbored the dream of creating an empire, and although his limited dominion among the nations was short lived, he still reigned for more than forty years as a powerful and illustrious sovereign. His appearance in scripture portrays him as a despotic ruler, yet one also at times who could be mild and temperate.

The prophet Jeremiah did not always approve of Nebuchadnezzar as a king, but he did accept him as a significant figure in the Middle East. Repeatedly he advised the kings of Judah to submit to Babylonian rule, not because of any righteousness or good character the Chaldeans might have had but merely because submission was a way to survive as a nation and culture. Had Judah submitted to the invaders, in other words, as the prophet counseled, the Jewish nation very likely would have continued until the time of Cyrus and the Persian Empire and consequently had a much different destiny as a people. It will always be ironic that Nebuchadnezzar's dream included the Kingdom of Judah, something which could have been a huge benefit to them if only they had been willing to cooperate and be a part of it.

Media

One of the mysterious figures in ancient history is Cyaxares who was king of the country called Media, a geographical area east of Mesopotamia that is now in Iran. About the same time that

Chaldea was rebelling against Assyria and becoming independent, Media was doing the same, and for a time the two states paralleled one another in their brief existence as independent nations.

Like Nebuchadnezzar, Cyaxares also dreamed of an empire, although one maybe not quite so extensive. Whereas the former coveted territory as far away as Egypt, the latter would liked to have had Asia Minor or what is now present-day Turkey. Neither ended up getting what he wanted, however, lasting fame eluding both of them as time ran out. Cyrus the Great of Persia eventually conquered the two nations and included them in an empire of his own.

But while Cyaxares was still king, he continued to pursue an elusive dream, particularly as he espied the fertile and prospective lands bordering on the Mediterranean. His vision unquestionably was toward the west, far from his natural homeland, and only a sudden eclipse of the sun which he interpreted as a foreboding omen finally caused him to return to Media.

Egypt

Psamtik I ruled Egypt for more than half a century and was succeeded by his son Necho. The new pharaoh was instantly confronted with the danger of his country being invaded, not only by advancing Medes and Chaldeans but also by the Scythians. His initial plan, therefore, was somehow to create a barrier between himself and the enemy.

In order to do this, he followed the example of his father by taking sides with Assyria, helping it to survive as a nation and thus providing the buffer zone he so desperately needed. At least this was his intention and indeed his dream.

But Egypt and Assyria together were defeated in battle, and had not Nebuchadnezzar and the Chaldeans unexpectedly returned to Babylon for the crown prince's coronation, the Medes going yet in another direction, things could have turned out badly for Necho. Fortune befriended him, however, and when he later repulsed the Chaldean armies at Migdol, at the very moment when they were about to enter Egypt, his dream of a favorable prospect for the future finally came true.

Greece

In Athens and throughout much of Greece, the poor people and those in the lower classes were in a pitiable condition when the man named Solon made his appearance in history. Among all who were in his time period, there were few who had a more specific goal and dream. Whatever his motive might have been at the time, he took a heroic stand and championed the cause of the common people, despite the fact that he himself was of the nobility.

By way of his office as archon in the Athenian government, Solon became known as a great liberator when he succeeded in freeing all those in Attica who were in slavery because of debt. He also secured legislation which removed any personal indebtedness, at the same time prohibiting anyone from offering himself or others as security for a loan. Moreover, he reduced the severity of civil and criminal laws and introduced various elements into the government that were more democratic.

Certainly he is recognized as one of those outstanding individuals who comes along from time to time and exerts a significant influence in the lives of men. As one of Lehi's most notable and well-known contemporaries, he fulfilled a dream by creating a free and more democratic society in Athens, as well as throughout Attica, causing the name of Solon to be forever associated with political wisdom and integrity.

Rome

As to when Rome was first established and came into existence as a city, there are different opinions, stories, and legends, but there is no question but what Lucius Tarquinius Priscus is one that might be considered its founder. He was the man who created not only political union and sovereignty in the Roman state but also an impressive civic image in the capital city through vast improvements and public works.

His notable accomplishment as an early leader and administrator was not just the founding of a city, if that is what it turns out to be, but injecting a new spirit into his particular time period and society, one that set the course of a people in an entirely new direction. Again it is possible that he is the specific person who originated the city of Rome and laid the foundation for the future Roman Empire.

Although many such statements and claims might be made, he is nevertheless an individual who had the potential to accomplish such a thing, as well as one having the visionary dream. His contribution to the culture and civilization of the 600 BC period was indeed a highly significant factor. Because of him a unique phenomenon took place in history, and at the end of his reign, a valuable legacy was left behind.

Lehi the Prophet

Among all those who participated in the drama of events occurring at the end of the seventh century BC and the beginning of the sixth, there is none more outstanding and important than the prophet Lehi. Especially because of his religious significance, there is no single person during his period of time that can equal him in importance, unless it is the unknown figure somewhere in the north countries who led the ten tribes to an unknown region. No other individual in so many ways, whether from

Judah, Assyria, Chaldea, or Media, can compare with him, nor from Egypt, Greece, or Rome. Regardless of what opinion others might have, the figure known as Lehi the Prophet can well be regarded as being unique among everyone else and considered as one of notability who stands alone.

And yet right behind him in a very meaningful way, according to the record in the Book of Mormon, was always the one called Nephi, both men acting in unison as father and son and each being instrumental in crossing a vast ocean to the American Continent and discovering a new world. Each man undoubtedly had a dream that in scope and significance was well beyond that of their contemporaries, and although they were unaware of any exact destination when they departed from Jerusalem in 600 BC, they soon learned that they were headed toward some kind of promised land.

Lehi also learned from genealogical records that he was a descendant of Joseph of Egypt and his son Manasseh. Because of this lineage he was the beneficiary of a patriarchal blessing bestowed upon Joseph by his father, Jacob, long ago which spoke of the branches of his posterity running over a wall.

"Joseph is a fruitful bough," Jacob told him, "even a fruitful bough by a well; whose branches run over the wall... The blessings of thy father have prevailed above the blessings of my progenitors unto the utmost bound of the everlasting hills: they shall be on the head of Joseph, and on the crown of the head of him that was separate from his brethren."[99]

At a later time, Moses pronounced a similar blessing on the entire tribe of Joseph as it was camped on the plains of Moab near Jericho. It was a blessing more extensive and detailed than that of any other tribe and once again spoke of a choice land that Joseph would someday inherit, one characterized by "ancient mountains" and "lasting hills."

"And of Joseph he said, Blessed of the Lord be his land, for the precious things of heaven, for the dew, and for the deep that coucheth beneath, and for the precious fruits brought forth by the sun, and for the precious things put forth by the moon, and for the chief things of the ancient mountains, and for the precious things of the lasting hills."[100]

Surely it was an interesting forecast, and especially for a man like Lehi who possibly had already traveled extensively as a merchant in the Middle East and along the Mediterranean. It was the type of blessing that undoubtedly started the prophet thinking. Yet even before he was called to the ministry, there might well have been some type of intimation or premonition that he would yet go to a more distant place, some feeling or silent whisper saying that an adventure of great magnitude lay just ahead which would take him and his family to a mysterious and unknown location.

For the prophet Lehi, as well as his devoted son Nephi, leaving the city of Jerusalem in 600 BC was indeed a historic occasion. Exactly six hundred years before the birth of Jesus Christ, as stated in ancient scripture, their departure became an important landmark of time and a pivotal date in history. Many centuries had passed since any known group had crossed the seas to the land of everlasting hills, and now a small caravan of Israelites who descended from Joseph was making the journey.

Again their specific destination was unknown, as were the specific reasons for going, but as the prophet and his family left the familiar environs of Jerusalem and headed into a vast desert, the whole world was before them and they did not hesitate. Indeed the future ahead was uncertain, and unseen circumstances awaited them, yet more than anything else Lehi trusted in a vision and a dream and believed that things would be all right, knowing that God himself would protect his people and throughout the long journey ahead be their guide!

References

600 b.c.

Note: The King James Version of the Bible, the Book of Mormon, the Doctrine and Covenants, and the Pearl of Great Price are standard works of The Church of Jesus Christ of Latter-day Saints.

1. 1 Nephi 19:8.
2. 1 Nephi 10:4.
3. 1 Nephi 2:5.
4. 1 Nephi 2:6–7.
5. Jeremiah 46:1–4, 9–10.
6. Daniel 1:1–2.
7. 2 Kings 24:2.
8. Jeremiah 25:4.
9. Jeremiah 26:9, 11.
10. Jeremiah 26:14–15.
11. Jeremiah 26:17.
12. Jeremiah 26:23.
13. Jeremiah 35:8–10, 17.
14. Jeremiah 36:2.
15. Jeremiah 36:5–6.
16. Jeremiah 36:15.
17. Jeremiah 36:23.
18. Jeremiah 36:30.

19. 2 Chronicles 36:6–7.
20. Daniel 1:4.
21. 2 Kings 24:12–16. Note: In his works, Josephus, the ancient Jewish historian, refers to 3,000 captives taken when Jehoiachin was made king and 10,000 three months later when he was replaced by Zedekiah (*Antiquities of the Jews,* Book 10, pages 272–273).
22. Jeremiah 22:11–12.
23. Jeremiah 22:19.
24. Jeremiah 22:24–26; 36:30.
25. 2 Kings 24:14.
26. Jeremiah 27:2–3, 12.
27. Jeremiah 27:6.
28. Jeremiah 27:11.
29. Jeremiah 27:12–13.
30. Jeremiah 51:64.
31. Jeremiah 29:5–7.
32. Jeremiah 29:10.
33. Jeremiah 28:16.
34. Jeremiah 21:2.
35. Jeremiah 21:4–6.
36. Jeremiah 21:8–10.
37. Jeremiah 37:3.
38. Jeremiah 37:7–10.
39. 1 Nephi 7:14.
40. Jeremiah 37:16–17.
41. Jeremiah 37:21.
42. Jeremiah 38:5.
43. Jeremiah 38:9.
44. Jeremiah 38:11–13.
45. Jeremiah 39:16–18.
46. Jeremiah 38:14.
47. Jeremiah 16.
48. Jeremiah 38:17.

49. Jeremiah 38:19–26.
50. Jeremiah 39:7; 2 Kings 35:7.
51. Ezekiel 17:15–19.
52. 2 Kings 25:9, 11–12.
53. Jeremiah 52:24–27.
54. 2 Kings 25:11–12.
55. Jeremiah 52:17–20; 25:13–16.
56. Jeremiah 39:13–14.
57. Jeremiah 39:12.
58. Jeremiah 40:2–5.
59. 2 Nephi 1:4.
60. Metzger, Bruce M. (Ed.). *Apocrypha of the Old Testament, Revised Standard Version*. New York: Oxford University Press, 1965, p. 65. Note: There are many things in the Apocrypha that have been declared to be true. (See Doctrine and Covenants 91:1–2.) The account pertaining to the ten tribes has often been used as a source of information but has not yet been completely verified.
61. Brough, R. Clayton. *The Lost Tribes*. Salt Lake City: Horizon Publishers, 1979, p. 44.
62. Doctrine and Covenants 133:26–27.
63. Doctrine and Covenants 133:30–34.
64. Metzger, Bruce M. (Ed.). *Apocrypha of the Old Testament, Revised Standard Version*. New York: Oxford University Press, 1965, p. 65.
65. 1 Nephi 22:3–4.
66. Jeremiah 52:9–10.
67. Omni 15–16.
68. Alma 22:30.
69. Helaman 6:10.
70. Doctrine and Covenants 133:26–27.
71. Conference Report of the Church of Jesus Christ of Latter-day Saints. Salt Lake City: The Church of Jesus Christ of Latter-day Saints, April 1916, p. 130.

72. Nahum 2:4; 3:1–3, 5, 7, 18–19.
73. Jeremiah 46:1–4.
74. Jeremiah 46:7–8.
75. Jeremiah 46:10.
76. Nahum 2:8, 10, 13.
77. Zephaniah 2:13–15.
78. Daniel 1:1–2.
79. Daniel 2:31.
80. Daniel 2:37.
81. Daniel 2:46–47.
82. Daniel 3:19–20.
83. Daniel 3:24–25, 27–29.
84. Jeremiah 27:6–7.
85. Jeremiah 51:37.
86. Jonah 1:2; 3:1–4; 4:11.
87. Genesis 11:4, 8.
88. 2 Kings 17:5–6.
89. Becking, Bob. *The Fall of Samaria, An Historical and Archeological Study.* Leiden: E. J. Brill, 1992, pp. 70–71; Oded, Bustenay. *Mass Deportations and Deportees in the Neo-Assyrian Empire* Wiesbaden, Germany: Ludwig Reichert Verlag, 1979, pp. 63–64.
90. Abraham 1:5–6, 16–17.
91. Webster, Richard (ed.). *The Volume Library.* New York: Educators Association, Inc., 1946, p. 2262.
92. 2 Kings 23:29.
93. 2 Chronicles 35:20–24.
94. Jeremiah 2:36.
95. Jeremiah 46:1–2.
96. Jeremiah 45:14.
97. Drydan, John (translator). Revised by Arthur Hugh Clough. *Plutarch's Lives.* New York: Random House, Inc., 1932, p. 100.

98. Hadas, Moses. *A History of Rome.* Gloucester, Massachusetts: Doubleday & Co., 1956, p. 100.
99. Genesis 49:22, 26.
100. Deuteronomy 33:13–15.

About the Author

Clay McConkie

Clay McConkie is a native of Utah. He is a teacher by occupation, having taught in the Salt Lake City schools for thirty years. He received a B.A. from Brigham Young University and a M.S. and Ph.D from the University of Utah. He and his wife reside in Provo, Utah, and are the parents of four children.

He is also the author of *One Flesh, The Gathering of the Waters, The Ten Lost Tribes, In Ephraim's Footsteps,* and *In His Father's Image.*

0 26575 79175 4